D1066556

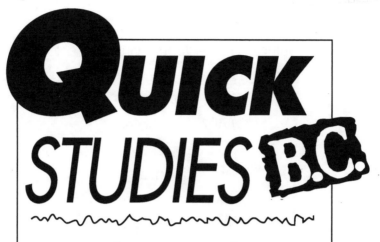

QUICK STUDIES B.C.

Joshua – Esther

Cook Ministry Resources
a division of Cook Communications Ministries
Colorado Springs, Colorado/Paris, Ontario

The following authors and editors contributed to this volume:

Stan Campbell
Mike Gillespie
Steve Hickey
Tim Richards
Randy Southern
Mark Syswerda
Rick Thompson
Jim Townsend, Ph.D.
Jane Vogel

Quick Studies B.C.
Joshua—Esther: The Books of History

© 1994 David C. Cook Publishing Co.

Cook Ministry Resources
a division of Cook Communications Ministries
4050 Lee Vance View, Colorado Springs, CO 80918-7100
Cable address: DCCOOK
Designed by Bill Paetzold
Cover illustrations by Mick Coulas
Inside illustrations by Scot Ritchie
Printed in U.S.A.

ISBN: 0-7814-5158-2

CONTENTS

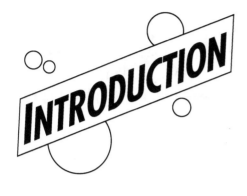

Quick Questions about Quick Studies

We've made *Quick Studies B.C.* as self-explanatory as possible, so you can dive in and start using them right away. But just in case you were wondering . . .

When should I use *Quick Studies B.C.*?
Whenever you want high school or junior high kids to explore the Bible face-to-face and absorb it into their lives. We've kept the openers active and the discussion questions creative, so you can use *Quick Studies B.C.* with confidence in Sunday school, midweek youth Bible study, small groups, even youth group meetings and retreats.

What's so quick about *Quick Studies B.C.*?
They're designed to save you preparation time. The session plans are compact, for quick reading. There aren't a lot of materials to gather, either (you'll need Bibles, pencils and paper, copies of the reproducible sheets, and sometimes a few other items). Yet *Quick Studies B.C.* are *real* Bible studies, with plenty of thought-provoking discussion and life application.

How are these different from other youth Bible studies?
We like to think *Quick Studies B.C.* are . . .
• *Irresistible.* You already know most kids don't jump at the chance to fill in a bunch of blanks in a boring study guide. So we used creative, reproducible sheets and *active* activities to draw kids into Scripture.
• *Involving.* You need discussion *starters*, not discussion *stoppers*. We avoided dull "yes or no" questions and included lots of thought-provokers that should get your group members talking about important issues. And we didn't forget suggested *answers* to most of the tougher questions, which should make things easier for you.
• *Inductive.* Many Bible studies try to force-feed kids a single "aim" and ignore other points Scripture is trying to make. *Quick Studies B.C.* let kids discover a variety of key principles in a passage.
• *Influential.* It's not enough to know what the Bible says. Every session includes a step designed to help kids decide what to do *personally* with vital points from the passage.

When do kids read the passages covered?
That's up to you. If your group is into homework, assign the
passages in advance. If not, take time to read the Scripture
together after the "Opening Act" step that kicks off each
session. There are dozens of ways to read a passage—with
volunteers taking turns, or with a narrator and actors "performing" a scene, or with kids underlining points as they read
silently, or with you reading as the author and kids listening
as the original audience, or with small groups paraphrasing as
they read . . .

**What if I want to cover more—or less—than a chapter in
a session?**
Quick Studies B.C. are flexible. Each 45- to 60-minute session covers a chapter of the Old Testament, but you can adjust
the speed to fit your group. To cover more than one passage
in a session, just pick the points you want to emphasize and
drop the activities, questions, and reproducible sheets you
don't need. To cover less than a chapter, you may need to add
a few questions and spend more time discussing the "So
What?" application step in detail.

Do I have to cover a whole Old Testament book?
No. Each session stands alone. Use sessions one at a time if
you want to, or mix and match books in any order you
choose. No matter how you use them, *Quick Studies B.C.* are
likely to help your group see Bible study in a whole new
light.

Randy Southern, Series Editor

JOSHUA 1

Captain Courageous

OVERVIEW

The Israelites are ready to enter the promised land after forty years of wandering in the desert. Moses has died; Joshua is appointed the new leader of the Israelites. However, before any battles for the promised land begin, Joshua must understand that God is the source of his strength and power.

OPENING ACT

(Needed: A room that can be locked with a key, a box, four slips of paper with Bible verses written on them)

Before the session, prepare four slips of paper. On each slip, write one of the following verses: Joshua 1:6; 1:7; 1:8; 1:9. Place the slips in a box. Then hide the box in a room that can be locked with a key. To begin the session, have kids form small groups. Give each group a key. (One of the keys should open the door of the box's hiding place.) Explain that a box is hidden somewhere in the building behind a locked door. The first group to find the box and bring it back to you unopened is the winner. Afterward, explain: **Inside this box is the key to Joshua's success when God called him to succeed Moses as leader of the Israelites. Just as there was one key to open the locked room, there was one key to Joshua's success. That key is also available to you.** Save the slips in the box to use later in the session.

DATE I USED THIS SESSION _____ GROUP I USED IT WITH _____

NOTES FOR NEXT TIME _____

_____

_____

1. What would you say is the most courageous thing you've ever done? What's the most courageous thing you've ever seen someone else do? Where does courage come from? Why do some people seem to be more courageous than others?

2. What qualifications do you think Joshua needed in order to succeed Moses as leader of the Israelites? (Most importantly, he had to be chosen by God. He probably also had to be strong, wise, trustworthy, and courageous. He also needed to be prepared to deal with a lot of whining.) **How do we know Joshua had such qualifications?** (God handpicked him to succeed Moses. Also, as Moses' assistant, Joshua probably had a good sense of what the job entailed.)

3. What do you think Joshua felt like doing after hearing God's promise to him (1:1-5)? (Perhaps he felt like praising God for giving him such incredible assurances. Perhaps he felt like "setting his foot" in as many places as possible as soon as possible [1:3].)

4. Open the shoebox you used in the "Opening Act" section. Hand out the slips to four group members. Instruct the kids to read the verses in order. **What was the key to Joshua's success as leader of the Israelites?** (Being strong, courageous, and grounded in God's law.) **Name some specific situations that Joshua might face that would require strength and courage.** (Battling the inhabitants of the promised land; acting as intermediary between God and the Israelites; confronting the Israelites when they sin; etc.)

5. Why was it so important for Joshua to meditate on the Book of the Law (1:1-5)? (When the Israelites followed God's law, God blessed them; when they disobeyed God's law, God punished them. In essence, God is saying, "All you have to do is follow the rules in this book to receive prosperity and success.") **Do you think meditating on God's Word *still* leads to prosperity and success? Why or why not?**

6. This is the second time the Israelites have been told to prepare to take possession of the promised land. See Numbers 13–14. **How does their response this time differ from

their first response? (This time, they do as they're commanded. The first time, they were so frightened by the inhabitants of the land that they threatened to stone anyone who suggested they try to take possession of Canaan.)

7. **Why do you think the Israelites were so willing to prepare to take possession of Canaan this time when they were so afraid to do it before?** (For one thing, this was a whole new generation of Israelites. The faithless generation had died out. Perhaps they were also trying to show their support for their new leader. But most likely, they remembered what the penalty was for not entering the promised land the first time.)

8. **The Israelites were given three days to prepare to take possession of the promised land. If you'd been among them, what kinds of things might you have thought about during those three days? Explain.**

9. **What do you think of the Israelites' pledge of allegiance in Joshua 1:16-18?** (The statement "Just as we fully obeyed Moses, so we will obey you" may not have been very reassuring to Joshua. After all, how often did the Israelites *fully* obey Moses?) **What do you think the odds are that the Israelites will *fully obey* Joshua? Explain.**

10. **Which passage, verse, or phrase in Joshua 1 means the most to you right now, at this point in your life? Why?**

Follow up the last question by focusing on some of the "key" principles of Joshua 1. Hand out copies of the reproducible sheet, "Keys to Victory." Ask group members to complete the statements inside each key. As they're working, encourage them to refer back to Joshua 1. When everyone is finished, ask volunteers to share their responses. Say: **God gave Joshua the key to victory in taking possession of the promised land. God gives each of us that same key.** Remind group members that the key to "victory" in life is being strong, courageous, and grounded in God's Word.

Keys to VICTORY

The situation I'm facing now that requires the most strength and courage is . . .

God used Joshua to lead the Israelites into the promised land. I think God might use me to . . .

Among the best direction and/or advice I've ever received from God's Word is . . .

One specific thing I can do to help others be strong and courageous is . . .

One specific thing I need to do in order to be more grounded in God's Word is . . .

The best leadership quality I have is . . .

JOSHUA 2

I Spy

Joshua has been given his marching orders and is readying the Israelites to take Canaan. He sends two spies into Jericho to "get the lay of the land." The spies stay in the house of a prostitute named Rahab. She hides the spies when the men of Jericho are looking for them. In return, the spies promise to spare Rahab and her family when the Israelites attack the city.

(Needed: Index cards)

Before the session, cut apart a copy of the reproducible sheet, "Spies Like Us." To begin the session, have kids form four teams. Give each team one of the cards from the sheet, a pencil, and three index cards. Explain that each team has been given a card with specific instructions on it. Team members must follow the instructions precisely. While they're doing so, they should also be spying on the other teams, trying to figure what the other teams' instructions are. When members of a team think they know the instructions of another team, they should write those instructions on one of their index cards. The first team to complete its instructions and figure out the instructions of the other teams is the winner. Afterward, ask: **Under what circumstances would you say it's OK to spy on someone?** Lead in to the story of Rahab and the spies.

DATE I USED THIS SESSION _____ GROUP I USED IT WITH _____

NOTES FOR NEXT TIME _____

_____

_____

1. What modern methods do people today use to spy on each other? Do you think you'd make a good spy? Why or why not?

2. God promised to give the land to the Israelites if they'd only take possession of it. So why do you think Joshua bothered sending spies into the land? (Perhaps he was plotting his military strategy to determine the most effective ways to attack the city.)

3. Why do you think the two spies decided to stay in the house of Rahab, a prostitute (2:1)? (Perhaps they thought no one would discover them if they stayed there. Perhaps they assumed that she wouldn't ask them any questions about where they came from or why they were in town.)

4. What did Rahab risk by hiding the spies? (If she'd been caught hiding the spies, it's likely that she and her whole family would have been put to death.) **What's the most you've ever risked to help someone else? Was it worth the risk? Why or why not?**

5. Do you think it was wrong for Rahab to tell a lie to the king of Jericho in order to save the two spies (2:4, 5)? Why or why not? Have you ever told a lie to protect someone else? If so, what were the circumstances? What was the result?

6. Why do you think Rahab risked so much to save the lives of two spies from an enemy nation? (She seems resigned to the fact that the Israelites will conquer the land of Canaan. She evidently sensed God's work on behalf of the Israelites.) **If you'd been in Rahab's position, what would you have done? Why?**

7. How did the Canaanites feel about the Israelites (2:8-11)? (The Canaanites were scared to death of the Israelites.) **Why do you suppose they felt this way?** (They had heard about the incredible things God had done for His people since they left Egypt. They had heard about the many battles the Israelites had won.) **What information do you suppose the spies included in their report on their mission?**

8. What favor did Rahab ask of the spies (2:12, 13)? (She requested that she and her entire family be spared when the Israelites invaded.) **Do you notice anything unusual about the request?** (Rahab seems to automatically assume that the Israelites will conquer Jericho.) **Do you think the Israelites had as much confidence that they would be victorious in Canaan as Rahab seemed to have? Why or why not?**

9. What stipulation did the spies put on their oath to Rahab? (They would spare her and her family *only* if she tied a red cord in the window of her house.) **What is the significance of this sign?** (The red cord may be reminiscent of the blood on the doorframes during the tenth plague—the death of the firstborn—in Egypt. In both cases, the people inside the marked house were spared.)

10. What are some ways in which God's people can be readily identified today? (By their attitudes, the way they treat others, their obedience to biblical commands, etc.)

11. How might this story have turned out differently if Rahab hadn't protected and hidden the Israelite spies? (God's will certainly still would have been done. Primarily, Rahab would have been the one to suffer. If she hadn't allied herself with God's people, she wouldn't have received God's mercy and blessings.) **What can we learn from this story about helping God's people?**

Point out that Rahab was an ancestor of Jesus (Matthew 1:5). Then have someone read aloud Hebrews 11:31. Ask: **According to this verse, what was the motive for Rahab's actions?** (Faith.) Ask your group members to silently consider what they could do in their community (or in the world) if they had the faith of Rahab. Then ask them to think of one thing they could do in the coming week to benefit God's people—perhaps helping with a church service project, tutoring younger kids in the church, or something else. Encourage them to follow Rahab's example and *get involved.*

SPIES LIKE US

Group #1

Your Task: One at a time, each group member will get a drink from a different water fountain (or faucet) in the building and then return to the group. But remember, at the same time you also have to figure out a way to spy on the other groups to figure out their assignments.

Group #2

Your Task: One at a time, each group member will remove his or her left shoe, take it to the restroom, leave it in the restroom waste basket, and return to the group. But remember, at the same time you also have to figure out a way to spy on the other groups to figure out their assignments.

Group #3

Your Task: One at a time, each group member will run (or walk) around the outside of the building and then return to the group. But remember, at the same time you also have to figure out a way to spy on the other groups to figure out their assignments.

Group #4

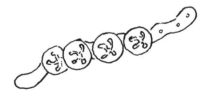

Your Task: One at a time, each group member will walk into another room, sit on the floor, sing "Jingle Bells" aloud, and then return to the group. But remember, at the same time you also have to figure out a way to spy on the other groups to figure out their assignments.

JOSHUA 5–6

Tumblin' Down

After miraculously crossing the Jordan River, the Israelites build a monument to commemorate the event. To reaffirm the Israelites' commitment to His covenant, God instructs that this new generation of Israelite males be circumcised. As the Israelites prepare for war, the commander of the Lord's heavenly armies comes to Joshua to lead the siege of Jericho. Meanwhile, the people of Jericho, who are terrified of the approaching Israelites, lock themselves in their walled cities. Once every day for six days, the Israelites (led by the ark of the covenant) march once around the city—with no one saying a word. Then on the seventh day, they march around the city seven times. On the seventh time around, the priests blow their trumpets and the people shout for joy—and the walls of Jericho come tumbling down. The Israelites destroy every living thing in the city, except for Rahab and her family.

Have kids form two teams. Instruct the members of one team to link arms to form an "impenetrable" circle. Explain that the goal of the linked team is to prevent anyone from entering the circle. The goal of the other team is to enter the circle. After a few minutes, have teams switch roles. Afterward, discuss the teams' strategies for entering an "impenetrable" area. Lead in to a discussion of the invasion of Jericho.

DATE I USED THIS SESSION _____ GROUP I USED IT WITH _____

NOTES FOR NEXT TIME _____

_____

_____

1. What's the largest thing you've ever seen destroyed? What was the destruction like? What is it about destruction that appeals to so many people?

2. If you had been a king living in Canaan, how would you have felt after hearing about the Jordan River incident (5:1)? Why? (Perhaps terrified, realizing that there's nothing you can do to stop the fast-approaching invaders.)

3. The Canaanite kings surely knew that when the Israelites tried to invade Canaan forty years earlier, they were soundly defeated (Numbers 14:39-45). So why do you think they were so worried about the Israelites this time? (Perhaps they sensed that this time the Lord was with them. Perhaps they had heard about the battles the Israelites had won in the past forty years.)

4. Why do you think God wanted Joshua to reinstate the rite of circumcision (Joshua 5:2-8)? (The original generation of the Israelite men of fighting age—who had been circumcised—had all died. Apparently, the people of Israel had not continued the practice of circumcision while wandering in the wilderness. Therefore, the new generation of Israelites was uncircumcised. To reaffirm the Israelites' commitment to His covenant, God instructed the Israelites to be circumcised.)

5. What do you think the commander of the Lord's army meant by his reply to Joshua (5:13-15)? (God was not "on the Israelites' side"; rather, the Israelites were fighting *God's* battles.)

6. When Joshua got his orders on how to conquer Jericho, what do you imagine he was thinking (6:1-7)? (Perhaps he thought it seemed like a weird way to fight a battle. Perhaps he was intrigued by the plan. More than likely, after seeing the miraculous ways in which the Lord had worked in the past, he was eager to get started and careful to follow God's plans exactly.)

7. Why do you think God wanted Joshua and the Israelites to conquer Jericho in this strange way? (Perhaps so they would know that the victory was God's doing and not theirs. Perhaps God was testing the people to see if they would follow His directions.)

8. If you had been a citizen of Jericho, what might you have been thinking as you watched the Israelites marching around your city day after day (6:8-16)? Why?

9. Imagine that you're a TV news reporter doing a live report from the top of one of Jericho's walls during the Israelites' seventh march around the city on the seventh day of the siege. What might your report be like?

10. What stipulations did the Lord place on the ransacking of Jericho (6:18, 19)? (The Israelites were not to take any "devoted thing" from the city—including silver, gold, and articles of bronze and iron.) Do you think this seems like an unreasonable request? Why or why not? (The Lord had given the Israelites the entire land of Canaan; they didn't need individual pieces of silver and gold.)

11. What became of Rahab the prostitute (6:25), who had hidden the Israelite spies when they came to "stake out" Jericho (2:1-21)? (She and all of her family were saved.) What can we learn from Rahab's experience about helping the Lord's people? (Eventually we will be rewarded for our actions.)

12. What can we learn from this story about facing obstacles in our life?

Hand out copies of the reproducible sheet, "Another Brick in the Wall," which asks group members to identify some of the barriers and obstacles they face in their relationship with God and then come up with an "equation" for "smashing through" the barriers and overcoming the obstacles. After a few minutes, ask for a couple of volunteers to share some of their barriers/obstacles and equations. Close the session in prayer, asking God to help your group members overcome the obstacles they face, just as He helped the Israelites topple the Jericho walls.

Another Brick in the Wall

We all face obstacles in life. The Israelites faced the Jericho walls; we face other kinds of "walls." And while the obstacles we face may not be fortified by armed men, they still can be just as imposing as the walls of Jericho.

In the bricks below, fill in some of the problems, situations, and circumstances that have become barriers or obstacles in your relationship with God.

In scientific/mathematical terms, God's equation for overcoming the walls of Jericho looks like this:

$$(am + 7tpp + AoC)(6[1wac] + 1[7wac]) + 1(ltb) + 1(lsbtI) = 0(Jw)$$

Key

am = *armed men*	tpp = *trumpet-playing priests*
AoC = *Ark of Covenant*	wac = *walk around city*
ltb = *long trumpet blast*	lsbtI = *loud shout by the Israelites*
Jw = *Jericho's walls*	

If you were to create a scientific/mathematical equation for overcoming the obstacles in your life, what would it be?

JOSHUA 7

The Cure for an Achan Heart

OVERVIEW

When the Israelites destroy Jericho, the Lord commands them not to take any of the "devoted things" of the city—the spoils of silver, gold, bronze, and iron—for themselves. They were to be given to God's treasury. Unfortunately, Achan disobeys God's command and secretly takes some booty for himself. As a result, the entire nation suffers. When the Israelites attack Ai, they are soundly defeated. This defeat shatters the Israelites' confidence. They begin to wonder if God is still with them. God tells Joshua that He will not be with the Israelites again until the guilty party is punished. After a process of elimination, Achan finally admits his sin. He and all of his family are then stoned to death.

OPENING ACT

Hand out copies of the reproducible sheet, "Guilty As Charged." Give group members a few minutes to complete the sheet. When everyone's finished, ask volunteers to share the sentences they came up with. Then, as a group, briefly discuss the concept of "the punishment fitting the crime." Lead in to a discussion of Achan's sin and punishment.

DATE I USED THIS SESSION _____ GROUP I USED IT WITH _____

NOTES FOR NEXT TIME _____

_____

_____

1. Have you ever gotten away with something you did wrong—at least for a little while? If so, how did you feel? What finally happened?

2. What do you think motivated Achan to take the forbidden things from Jericho (7:1)? (Perhaps he thought he could get away with it, if no one saw him. Perhaps he was so motivated by greed that he didn't think about the consequences of his actions.)

3. How did the Israelites seem to feel about taking possession of Ai (7:2, 3)? (They were so confident of victory that they sent only three thousand men to battle.) **Why do you think they felt that way?** (Perhaps Ai was a small, relatively unprotected city. Perhaps the Israelites were brimming with confidence after their decisive victory at Jericho.)

4. How do you think the Israelites felt after the men of Ai "routed" them in battle (7:4, 5)? (Perhaps they questioned whether God was still with them or not. Perhaps they started to feel vulnerable, as though they might be attacked by other Canaanite groups.)

5. How do you think Joshua felt after the defeat at Ai (7:6-9)? (Obviously, he was distressed. Perhaps he thought *he* had done something wrong in leading the Israelites across the Jordan. He wanted to know what he had to do to regain the Lord's favor for Israel.)

6. Why was it important for the Israelites to consecrate themselves (7:13)? (They were getting ready to attend an assembly called by the Lord.) **Do you do anything to prepare yourself before you meet with the Lord in prayer or worship? If so, what? If not, why not?**

7. Describe what you think the "elimination process" for determining the guilty party was like (7:14-18). **If you'd been one of the Israelites, how would you have felt while waiting for your clan's name to be called? What do you think Achan was thinking during this process?**

8. **How do you think the rest of the Israelites felt after hearing Achan's confession?** (Perhaps some of them felt relief, knowing that the guilty party had been identified. Perhaps others were angry at Achan for causing them to suffer because of his sin. Perhaps others were glad that they'd resisted the temptation to do as Achan had done.)

9. **What do you think of God's punishment of Achan (7:22-26)? Does it seem too severe to you? Why or why not?**

10. **Describe a time in your life when you broke a rule and had to face a tough consequence for it. What happened? How did you feel about the consequence at the time? How do you feel about it now?**

Say: **Achan confessed his sin, but was still killed for it. Do you think that's fair? Why or why not?** Help group members see that confessing sin and asking God's forgiveness does not automatically spare us from facing the consequences of our actions. Take another look at the reproducible sheet. As a group, discuss the consequences for the people who did wrong, the consequences for those who were wronged, and any other consequences that resulted from the actions. Ask: **What if no one found out about these wrongdoings? Would any of the consequences have changed? If so, how?** Close the session with a time of silent prayer, giving group members an opportunity to confess any wrongs they've committed. Then wrap up the prayer time by asking God to give group members the strength and courage to face the consequences of any sinful actions.

Read the following cases and come up with an appropriate sentence for each "crime."

Case #1
THE CRIME: Rico needs at least a "C" in his math class in order to stay on the soccer team. If he can stay on the team, he's almost assured of making the all-conference team. And if he makes the all-conference team, he'll probably attract some college scouts—college scouts who may be offering scholarships. So Rico cheats on one of his math tests. Unfortunately, during the test, his "cheat sheet" falls out of his sleeve and onto the floor—where it is picked up by the teacher.

The Sentence:

Case #2
THE CRIME: To make some quick money, Geoff swipes a bottle of vodka from his parents' liquor cabinet and sells it to an eleven-year-old kid down the street. The kid's mom finds out about it and calls Geoff's parents.

The Sentence:

Case #3
THE CRIME: Jocelyn lies to her best friend, telling her that she can't go to the mall with her tonight because she isn't feeling well. Jocelyn then goes out with some other friends to see a movie. The next day, Jocelyn's best friend finds out the truth.

The Sentence:

Case #4
THE CRIME: Ben is in eighth grade. One of his mom's rules is that Ben is not allowed to ride in a car with a teenage driver. On the way home from school one day, Ben's best friend's sixteen-year-old brother offers Ben a ride home. Not wanting to be rude, Ben accepts, figuring his mom may not be home when he gets there. Unfortunately, when the car pulls up in front of Ben's house, Ben's mom is standing outside.

The Sentence:

JOSHUA 10

Don't Let the Sun Go Down on Us

In a second attack on Ai, the Israelites emerge victorious. When the Gibeonites hear what the Israelites have done at Jericho and Ai, they trick Joshua into making a peace treaty, thus saving their city. Five Amorite kings hear about the Gibeonites' plan and decide to attack the "traitors." The Gibeonites plead with Joshua to save them, so the Israelites engage in a battle with the Amorite kings. During the battle, God stops the sun to allow enough daylight to complete the victory. The Israelites press on, taking possession of the cities in the promised land and destroying their inhabitants.

Hand out copies of the reproducible sheet, "It's All in the Timing." Give kids a few minutes to complete the sheet. Then go through the sheet one question at a time, asking kids to call out their responses. Allow some time for kids to challenge each other's responses. If possible, you might want to time kids as they perform some of the actions on the sheet. Afterward, ask: **How long do you think it would take the Israelites to defeat another nation in battle?** The answer is "About one day—if the sun stands still while you fight."

DATE I USED THIS SESSION _____ GROUP I USED IT WITH _____

NOTES FOR NEXT TIME _____

_____

_____

1. Think of the longest day of your life. What was it like? What happened to make it seem so long? How do you handle days like that?

2. Think of a day that you wish had lasted forever. What was it like? How did you feel when the day ended? Why?

3. Why do you think the five Amorite kings were angry with the Gibeonites (10:1-5)? (Perhaps they were upset at having been betrayed. Perhaps they were counting on the Gibeonites' help in defending themselves against the Israelites. After all, the men of Gibeon "were good fighters" [10:2].) Have you ever had one of your friends "get friendly" with an enemy of yours? If so, how did you feel? Have you ever "gotten friendly" with an enemy of one of your friends? If so, why?

4. The people of Gibeon tricked the Israelites into signing a peace treaty with them (9:3-15). So why do you think Joshua was willing to come to the aid of these people (10:6, 7)? (He had made a treaty with them and was bound to honor it. Perhaps he thought it would be easier battling five armies who were all together at the same time—a "kill five birds with one stone" mentality.)

5. Have you ever come to the aid of someone who was seriously outnumbered—or perhaps facing incredible odds? If so, why did you do it? What happened? Has anyone ever come to your aid when you were seriously outnumbered? If so, what happened? How did you feel?

6. Joshua 10:11 tells us that the hailstones killed more Amorites than the Israelites did. Why do you think this is important to note? (This proves that the victory wasn't the Israelites'; it was God's.)

7. It took a lot of confidence for Joshua to ask God to make the sun stand still so the Israelites could finish battling the Amorites (10:12, 13). What do you think gave Joshua this confidence? (God had already promised to give the Amorites into the Israelites' hands [10:8].) What's the biggest thing you've ever prayed for? What happened?

8. If you'd been one of the Israelites, how would you have felt when the sun stood still for you? (Perhaps happy to be on God's side and confident of victory.) **If you'd been one of the Amorites, waiting for night to fall so you could get away from the Israelites, how would you have felt when the sun stood still?** (Perhaps doomed, realizing that even the elements of nature were against you.)

9. What do you think of the punishment of the five Amorite kings who opposed Israel (10:16-28)? Explain.

10. What does the account of the five Amorite kings tell you about opposing God and His people? (Those who oppose God and His people will eventually be punished accordingly.)

11. What do you think of Israel's invasion of the promised land? After all, not only were the Israelites taking over other nations, they were also killing everyone in those cities. If no one mentions it, point out that Canaan rightfully belonged to the Israelites. God had promised it to them. So they were actually driving other people out of *their* (the Israelites') land. In killing the people of the other nations, they were acting as agents of God's judgment. They were punishing the people for their wickedness.

Have someone read aloud Matthew 17:20, 21 and John 14:12-14. Say: **Joshua prayed that the sun would stand still—and it did. Jesus says that faith as small as a mustard seed can move mountains. He also says that if we ask for anything in His name, He will do it for us. Do you pray like you believe these things? If not, why not?** Remind your group members that they're praying to the same God who performed unbelievable miracles for the Israelites. Emphasize that He's ready to help us too—if we ask according to His will (I John 5:14, 15). Give your group members an opportunity to write down some prayer requests they'd like to take to God. Then encourage kids to start a regular prayer time—a time in which they bring not only their requests to God, but their praise and worship as well.

IT'S ALL IN THE TIMING

1. *How long* would it take you to drink a can of soda if you were really thirsty?

2. *How long* would it take you to finish a box of your favorite cereal if you were really hungry?

3. *How long* would it take you to run around the bases on a regulation-size baseball diamond?

4. *How long* would it take you to read the Book of Psalms in the Old Testament?

5. *How long* would it take you to read the Book of III John in the New Testament?

6. *How long* would it take you to make your best friend really angry if you wanted to?

7. *How long* would it take you to get a job if you started trying right this minute?

8. *How long* would it take you to walk home right now?

9. *How long* would it take you to name the Seven Dwarfs?

10. *How long* would it take you to earn $100?

11. *How long* would it take you to hit five free throws in a row?

12. *How long* would it take you to do fifty situps?

13. *How long* would it take you to type five hundred words?

14. *How long* would it take you to make a paper airplane?

15. *How long* would it take you to sing "Happy Birthday to You" as fast as you can five times?

JOSHUA 23–24

Don't Forget!

The Israelites settle into Canaan and claim it as their own. Each tribe is allocated its own land, though some territory remains to be taken. A brief misunderstanding occurs when three of the tribes build an altar on the border of Canaan. Thinking the altar is to a pagan god, the other tribes send a delegation to rebuke the "wayward" tribes. However, the delegation discovers that the altar was built to God Himself. By this time, Joshua is old and close to death. Like Moses before him, Joshua gives a farewell address in which he urges the Israelites to continue to obey God's law and not to inter-marry with the surrounding heathen nations. After renewing God's covenant with the Israelites, Joshua dies.

(Needed: Video equipment, videotapes [optional])

If possible, play some video clips of famous "good-bye scenes" (which you've screened beforehand). Among the movies you might use are *Casablanca* and *Gone with the Wind.* If you can't show video clips, ask kids to describe their favorite good-bye scenes from movies or TV shows. You might also have kids form teams for a contest to see who can come up with the most ways to say good-bye. Point out that in this session, Joshua says good-bye to the people of Israel.

DATE I USED THIS SESSION _____ GROUP I USED IT WITH _____

NOTES FOR NEXT TIME _____

_____

_____

1. Have you ever had to say good-bye to a friend or family member, knowing that you wouldn't see that person again for a long, long time? If so, what was it like? What did you say to the person?

2. When Joshua gathered the leaders of Israel together, what were some of the things he commanded them to do (23:6-13)? (Obey God's commands in the Book of the Law; do not associate with idolatrous nations; do not intermarry with foreigners.)

3. If you had been one of the leaders of Israel listening to Joshua at this time, what might you have been thinking? Why?

4. How do you think the leaders might have reacted to Joshua's stern prediction that God would take back the land if the Israelites broke His covenant (23:14-16)? Why?

5. Have you ever received a stern warning from a parent or someone else, but then gone against it anyway? If so, why? What happened?

6. Why do you think Joshua chose to review the history of Israel before his death (24:1-13)? (Perhaps to give the Israelites the "big picture" of what God had done for them.) If you'd been one of the Israelites listening to Joshua's "history lesson," which incidents do you think would have meant the most to you? Why?

7. Why do you think Joshua wanted the Israelites to make a decision one way or the other about whom they would serve (24:14, 15)? (Perhaps he wanted to "weed out" the faithful from the unfaithful. Perhaps he wanted to give the Israelites an opportunity to make a conscious decision about whom they would serve [on the principle that "If you don't stand for something, you'll fall for anything"].)

8. What do you think of Joshua's statement "As for me and my household, we will serve the Lord" (24:15)? How would you have felt if you'd been one of Joshua's children? Do you think parents have the right to determine how their children will worship? Why or why not?

9. Why do you think Joshua questioned the Israelites after they announced that they would serve the Lord (24:16-24)? (Perhaps he wanted them to completely consider the matter before answering.)

10. Why do you think Joshua sealed the people's promise that day with a special covenant (24:19-27)? (Perhaps to give them a constant reminder of what they had pledged.)

11. Why do you think there was no designated leader after Joshua? (Perhaps because since the Israelites had taken possession of the land, God was to be their leader.)

12. What epitaph would you put on Joshua's grave? Why?

Hand out copies of the reproducible sheet, "Graduation Advice." Give group members a few minutes to work on it. When everyone is finished, ask volunteers to share what they wrote. Compare your group members' advice with the advice given by Joshua at the end of his life. Point out that the key to success and happiness for us today is the same as the key for the Israelites—loving God, obeying God's commands, and remaining faithful to Him.

Graduation Advice

You've just been selected to write a letter to your graduating class. Fill in this document with the advice you would share to encourage others to be happy and successful in life.

To the members of the Class of _____ :

It is a privilege to write this graduation letter to you. I particularly want to thank
_____
_____

As we prepare to leave this school, I think the most important thing we've learned is that
_____
_____

One piece of advice my parent(s) gave me that might apply to you, too, is
_____
_____

I believe that success is available to all of us if we _____
_____

Sometimes we'll face disappointments. The best way I know of to cope with disappointment is
_____
_____

One of the keys to a successful life is having the right friends. And one of the most important things to remember when it comes to friends is _____
_____
_____

God's advice for us at this time in our lives is _____
_____

I wish each of you the best.

Sincerely,

JUDGES 2–3

Here Come the Judges

After Joshua's death, the Israelites continue to take possession of the promised land. However, they fail to obey God's command to drive all of the Canaanites and their pagan gods out of the land. As a result, God removes His hand of blessing from the people. Thus begins a dreary cycle: the Israelites disobey God by worshiping false gods that stood for immoral practices; God allows an enemy of the Israelites to conquer them; the Israelites cry to God for help; God raises up a judge (or a military leader) to lead the Israelites to freedom; the Israelites disobey God again. Othniel, Ehud, and Shamgar are three of the judges God raises up. Although little information is given regarding Othniel and Shamgar, Ehud makes his mark in history by burying his sword in the belly of the obese Eglon, king of Moab.

Hand out copies of the reproducible sheet, "Mortal Combat." Give group members a few minutes to work. When everyone is finished, have group members check their answers with Judges 3:12-30. Use this activity to introduce the period of the judges of Israel.

DATE I USED THIS SESSION _____ GROUP I USED IT WITH _____

NOTES FOR NEXT TIME _____

_____

_____

1. After all God had done for them, why do you suppose the people of Israel turned away from God (2:1-3)? (Temptation was all around them in the form of foreign "gods" [2:13]. The people who had seen God's miracles in Egypt had all died, leaving only "second generation" inhabitants of the promised land [2:7, 10].)

2. What things cause people—especially young people—today to turn away from God? Explain.

3. Would you describe yourself more as someone who has "seen all the great things the Lord [has] done" (2:7) or someone who "[knows] neither the Lord nor what he [has] done" (2:10)? Explain. (Even though none of us saw God's miracles in Egypt or walked with Jesus face-to-face as the disciples did, every Christian can claim firsthand knowledge of God and experience His working through the Holy Spirit. But people who haven't accepted a personal relationship with Jesus may feel like the "second generation" Israelites.)

4. What can we learn about God from the way He responded to Israel during the time of the judges? (God takes disobedience seriously—He allowed Israel to be conquered by her enemies. But He is also compassionate and forgiving, as He showed by "bailing out" the Israelites time after time after time. Note the cycle of sin, punishment, crying out to God, and deliverance.)

5. How does God deliver us today? See Judges 3:9, 15. (Jesus is, of course, the ultimate Deliverer, who saves us from our sins and brings us into relationship with God. But God also uses ordinary people to help us resist temptation and grow in faith. And every Christian has the Holy Spirit to equip him or her for battle, just as the judges were equipped [3:10].)

6. If you were making a movie about Ehud, what parts of the story would you highlight? What would you call your movie? Who would you cast as Ehud? Why? Who would you cast as Eglon? Why? What would your movie be rated? Why?

7. **Why do you suppose the Bible tells us that Ehud was left-handed** (3:15)**?** (Perhaps since most people are right-handed, Eglon might have been watching Ehud's right hand for any sudden moves. Perhaps that's why he was unprepared for Ehud to pull a sword with his left hand.)

8. **What other qualities did Ehud have that equipped him to defeat Israel's enemies?** (He was brave, he took the initiative, he came up with a good plan, he knew his enemy's weakness, he motivated others, he trusted and gave credit to God.)

9. **Just for fun: How long do you think Eglon's servants waited before unlocking the door** (3:24, 25)**?**

10. **What are some "enemies" you might face as you try to stay faithful to God?**

11. **What qualities or resources do you have that God can use to help you fight these enemies?** (Christian friends to do fun things with; a longing to know God better; the Bible; the Holy Spirit.)

(Needed: Markers)

Say: **Ehud's left-handedness was a distinctive strength he used to overcome his enemy.** Hand out markers (making sure their ink washes off easily). Continue: **Everyone here has certain distinctive strengths that can help overcome the enemies we discussed earlier. Grab somebody's left hand. Write on that person's hand a positive distinctive strength you see in that person. Think of personal qualities like determination or sense of humor as well as abilities like intelligence or athletic skill.** Have group members continue until everyone has at least six things written on his or her hand. Circulate and direct kids toward those who need things written on their hands. Then say: **When we rely on God to help us use our strengths, we'll find out that our enemies are easier to overcome than we first thought.**

Mortal Combat

Circle the option you choose for each of the following screens. When you're finished, check your responses to see how well they compare with the story in Judges 3:12-29.

1

Warning: This game contains scenes of violence. It is not intended for small children or squeamish adults.

EHUD vs. EGLON

2

Choose your weapon.

3

Choose your method of escape.

4

GAME OVER

JUDGES 4–5

Sisera's Headache

OVERVIEW

After the death of Ehud, Deborah becomes judge of Israel. She brings a message from God to Barak, an Israelite military man, that God has promised to lure the Canaanites into defeat at Barak's hands. Barak balks at his assignment, agreeing to fight only if Deborah will go with him. God keeps His promise. But because of Barak's unwillingness, the credit for the victory goes not to Barak, but to a woman named Jael, who pounded a stake through the head of the enemy commander, Sisera, as he lay sleeping in her tent. Deborah commemorates the victory with a song, giving the ultimate credit to God.

OPENING ACT

Read the following "minute mystery" scenario: **Tom stepped out onto his patio one evening and nearly tripped over a dead body. "I'm going to put a stop to this senseless dying," he exclaimed. So he went inside and pulled the drapes. Why did he do that?** Let kids ask questions that can be answered "yes" or "no" to try to solve the mystery. Answer the questions honestly based on this solution: **The body was that of a bird that had flown into the sliding glass door, not realizing it was glass. Tom drew the drapes so that other birds would not make the same mistake.** Afterward, point out that this session contains the story of another bizarre death, with an unexpected twist to it.

DATE I USED THIS SESSION _____ GROUP I USED IT WITH _____

NOTES FOR NEXT TIME _____

_____

_____

1. Have you ever been told to do something that seemed beyond your abilities? If so, what were the circumstances? What happened? Would you have felt any more confident if you'd had someone helping or accompanying you? Explain.

2. What kinds of things do you think Deborah would put on her resumé? Why?

3. Why do you think Barak was hesitant in doing what the Lord commanded (4:6-8)? (Perhaps he was aware of the strength of Sisera's army. After all, Sisera had nine hundred iron chariots and a twenty-year history of supremacy.) **If you had been Barak, what would you have done? Why?**

4. Why do you think Barak refused to go to battle without Deborah? (Perhaps he wasn't aware of God's strength and the way God works. Perhaps he assumed that God's promise would apply only if Deborah were present.)

5. How do you think Barak felt when Deborah told him that the honor for the victory would go to a woman instead of to him? (He may have been angry with himself for not obeying right away. Perhaps he was ashamed that a "mere woman" would get the glory he could have had. Perhaps he assumed that Deborah was the woman who would kill Sisera.)

6. If you were filming this story for a TV miniseries, what elements in Judges 4:11-24 would you focus on to build suspense? (You could cut away to the apparently irrelevant campsite of Heber the Kenite [4:11] to make the viewer wonder what might happen there. You could slowly pan across Sisera's nine hundred iron chariots [4:13], emphasizing the strength of Israel's foes. You could make a dramatic scene out of Deborah's telling Barak, "Go!" [4:14]. You could make quite a chase scene out of verses 15 and 16. You could play up Sisera's escape [4:17] and refuge in Jael's tent [4:18].)

7. Why do you suppose Jael's giving Sisera milk was important enough to merit mention in Deborah's victory song (5:25)? (It shows Jael's cleverness in lulling Sisera into a false sense of security. It may even have been a strategic move to help Sisera get to sleep better, just as mothers give their children warm milk at bedtime. It heightens the drama because it really does seem like Jael is on Sisera's side.)

8. **What do you think went through Barak's mind when he came to Jael's tent and she led him inside (4:22)?** (Perhaps he was exultant about finding his enemy. Perhaps he expected a duel with Sisera, thinking he might be the one to get Sisera after all. Perhaps he was dumbfounded to see that a hospitable woman had accomplished the greatest victory of the battle.)

9. **Who do you most identify with in this story: Deborah, the motivator; Barak, the reluctant; or Jael, the unlikely warrior? Why? Who do you think is the champion of the story? Explain.**

10. **What do you think is the purpose of Deborah's song?** (Perhaps to focus attention on God's role in the victory and give Him praise. Perhaps to retell the story for people who used songs and storytelling, not textbooks, to learn history.)

11. **How do you respond when you've accomplished something good? How do you celebrate? How do you give God credit?**

Hand out copies of the reproducible sheet, "Triumph Song." Read aloud the directions and the sample song on the sheet. Then encourage group members to work individually to create their own songs of praise for something good that has happened in their lives.

TRIUMPH SONG

What do you do when something goes right?
Take a tip from Deborah: try writing a song of praise
to God about it. Notice how Deborah did it:

• *She sang about a specific event. What specific event in the last week*
  or two are you glad about?

• *She celebrated her own accomplishments. What accomplishment*
  would you celebrate?

• *She celebrated the accomplishments of others. Did other people*
  play a part in your accomplishment? If so, what did they do?

• *She gave praise to God. What did God do to make your accomplishment possible?*

To give some form to your "song," start each line with the letters below. Don't worry about rhyming—a lot of great poetry doesn't rhyme. If you're really good, try ending some sentences somewhere other than the end of each line.

Here's an example to get you started:

> **T**oday I aced a test.
> **R**ight after school
> **I** rushed home to tell my mom.
> **U**p all night studying the night before,
> **M**y head swimming with facts, I asked God:
> **P**lease help me!
> **H**e did!

Now you try.

T

R

I

U

M

P

H

JUDGES 6–8

The Fleece Circus

As punishment for the Israelites' return to idol worship, God allows the Midianites to overrun Israel. Later, the angel of the Lord appears to Gideon, promising him victory over the Midianites. Gideon, an unlikely military leader, needs some assurance, so twice he asks God to give him a sign. Once convinced, Gideon demonstrates God's power, defeating the Midianites with an army of three hundred men.

Cut apart two copies of the reproducible sheet, "A Winning Hand," for each group member. Have kids sit in a circle. Deal seven cards to each person. Turn one of the remaining cards faceup; stack the rest facedown. The first player must put a card of the same color or number on the faceup card. If the person can't match the card, he or she must draw one card and lose the turn. A "Skip" card means the person to the player's left is skipped. A "Draw 2" card means the person to the player's left must draw two cards. A "Reverse" card changes the direction of play, with the person on the player's *right* playing the next card. A "Wild" card may be used for any color or number. Play until one person is out of cards. The remaining players add up their points, with least points being the best score. Afterward, say: **Sometimes less is more. Let's see how God made winners out of a few soldiers.**

DATE I USED THIS SESSION _____ GROUP I USED IT WITH _____

NOTES FOR NEXT TIME _____

_____

_____

Q&A

1. **What circumstances today might cause people to say, "The Lord has abandoned us"** (6:13)? (Random violence, devastating illness, poverty, divorce, failing at school no matter how hard you try, etc.)

2. **Why do you think God continuously reminds the Israelites of everything He's done for Israel in the past** (6:7-10)? (Perhaps the Israelites really had forgotten what the Lord had done for their ancestors. Perhaps God was showing the Israelites that He was capable of helping them again if they turned from their wicked ways.)

3. **Why might Gideon be nominated as a candidate for "Least Likely Warrior"?** (He was the youngest son in the weakest clan of the half-tribe of Manasseh.) **So why do you think God chose Gideon to lead the Israelites?** (Perhaps to show that the victory belonged to Him [God] alone, and not to some great human leader.)

4. **If God came to you with a big job to do, what things might make you feel inadequate, as Gideon did** (6:15)? (Perhaps being too young; not being smart enough; being too shy; not being a "leader type"; etc.)

5. **What was the first thing Gideon did after the Lord spoke with him** (6:17, 18)? (He prepared an offering for God to worship Him.) **What can we learn about Gideon from this?** (Even though he was bold enough to ask God for a sign, he was humble enough to worship God. When he was unsure about what to do, he turned to God in worship.)

6. **Gideon was afraid to tear down the idol altars during the day, so he did it at night** (6:27). **When have you felt afraid or embarrassed about something you knew was right to do?** (Praying before a meal in front of classmates at school; speaking out against things that are wrong like crude joking, lying, and gossiping; etc.)

7. **The Israelites called Gideon "Jerub-Baal" because he tore down Baal's altars** (6:32). **What nickname would indicate a strength that you have or refer to something**

courageous you've done? Explain. ("Gossip Stopper"? "Friendmaker"? "Cares about Children"?)

8. **If you'd been Gideon, how do you think you would have felt as God made your army smaller and smaller? Why?**

9. **If you'd been a member of Gideon's army, which group would you have been a part of? Would you have been one of the twenty-two thousand "tremblers"** (7:3)? **Would you have been one of the ninety-seven hundred "kneelers"** (7:6)? **Or would you have been one of the three hundred fighters** (7:8)? **Explain.**

10. **What "enemy" are you facing that seems to have larger forces than yours? What will it take to give you the courage to go to war against that enemy?**

11. **What have you learned from Gideon's story that gives you confidence for your own battles?** (God can use us even though we don't feel very impressive. God's power is stronger than any enemy. God wants us to trust Him. We need to listen to God more.)

12. **It's your job to create a Gideon trading card. What picture would you put on the front of the card? Why? What vital information would you include on the back? Why? What were Gideon's strengths and weaknesses?**

Hand out the cards from the reproducible sheet again. Have kids sort through and trade cards until everyone has one complete set of the cards numbered 1 through 5. As a group, read through each sentence, look up the Scripture passage listed, and discuss how God helped Gideon deal with the feeling or need. Encourage kids to take the cards home and look at them when they need encouragement.

A WINNING HAND

When you feel as if God has left you, remember, Gideon thought so too—but God stuck with him (Judges 6:12, 13).

When you feel inadequate, remember, Gideon was an unlikely hero too (Judges 6:15, 16).

When you need to know that God is with you, first worship Him, as Gideon did (Judges 6:17, 18).

When you're afraid to stand up for your faith, remember, so was Gideon—but God helped him (Judges 6:25-32).

When you feel overwhelmed, remember, God shows His power through human weakness (Judges 7).

SKIP
(10 points)

DRAW 2
(10 points)

WILD
(10 points)

REVERSE
(10 points)

JUDGES 10–11

The Agony of Victory

After Gideon's death, the Israelites once again turn to idol worship. As a result, they endure eighteen years of oppression from the Philistines and Ammonites. Then God raises up Jephthah to lead Israel against the Ammonites. Jephthah makes a rash vow that if God gives him victory against the Ammonites, Jephthah will sacrifice the first thing to greet him when he returns home. When Jephthah returns home victorious, the first thing to greet him is his only daughter. So Jephthah sadly fulfills his vow.

In small groups, have kids respond to the following questions:
• **If you could become very wealthy, but had to give up your best friend to do it, would it be worth it? Why or why not?**
• **If you could become the most attractive person in the world, but would only live to be thirty-five, would it be worth it? Why or why not?**
• **If you could become successful and famous in your chosen career, but could never marry or have a romantic relationship, would it be worth it? Why or why not?**

Afterward, explain that Jephthah was a judge who paid a high price for his success.

DATE I USED THIS SESSION _____ GROUP I USED IT WITH _____

NOTES FOR NEXT TIME _____

_____

_____

1. How do you explain the Israelites' pattern of rebelling against God, being oppressed by other countries as a result, crying out to God to save them, and then forgetting about God when things are going well again? Can you think of any modern-day parallels?

2. How do you suppose Jephthah felt when his brothers drove him away (11:1, 2)? (Perhaps embarrassed, rejected, and bent on revenge.) **Why?**

3. What kinds of things cause people to be rejected or looked down upon today?

4. Why do you think the elders of Gilead asked Jephthah to lead the fight against the Ammonites (11:4-6)? (Perhaps Jephthah and his band of "adventurers" [11:3] had become experts in guerilla warfare.)

5. If you had been Jephthah, how would you have responded when the people who had rejected you later came to you for help?

6. Why do you think Jephthah sent a correspondence to the king of the Ammonites before the two nations went to war (11:12-28)? (Perhaps he wanted to see if war with the Ammonites could be avoided. Perhaps he wanted to establish specific grounds for war.)

7. If you had been king of the Ammonites, how would you have responded to Jephthah's message in Judges 11:15-27? Why?

8. Why do you suppose Jephthah made the vow he did (11:30, 31)? (Scripture doesn't tell us, but it seems possible that Jephthah was so eager to maintain his newfound status that he would gamble anything.)

9. Do you think God helped Jephthah win the battle because of his vow? Why or why not? (Although the writer of Judges doesn't condemn Jephthah's vow in this passage, God had previously made it clear to His people that He detests human sacrifice [Deuteronomy 12:31]. God had already established the pattern of saving the Israelites because of their repentance, so a more appropriate vow might have been to offer a sacrifice of gratitude and give God the glory after the victory, as Deborah did [Judges 5]. Note that God takes vows seriously [Numbers 30:2; Deuteronomy 23:21-23].)

10. **What are people willing to sacrifice today to get what they want?**

11. **What have you learned from Jephthah's story that you can apply the next time you want God's help? Explain.** (There's no need to try to bargain with God. We should beware of asking for things to make us look important.)

Hand out copies of the reproducible resource sheet, "Open Mouth, Insert Foot." Give group members a few minutes to work. When everyone is finished, ask volunteers to share and explain the comic strips they created. Then have someone read aloud Proverbs 10:19; 20:25. Ask: **If you had to sum up the principles in these verses in two sentences, how would you do it?** Close the session in prayer, asking God to help your group members think before they speak.

OPEN MOUTH, INSERT FOOT

Read the following comic-strip account of Jephthah's foolish vow. Then create your own comic strip, detailing an incident in which you (or someone you know) said something that later came back to haunt you (or him or her).

JUDGES 13–15

The Riddler

After Jephthah defeats the Ammonites, the Ephraimites get angry because they weren't asked to go to battle. The skirmish develops into a "mini-civil war" between Jephthah's army and the Ephraimites. As a result, forty-two thousand Ephraimites are killed. After Jephthah dies, a succession of judges leads Israel. When the Israelites revert back to their wicked ways, the Lord allows the Philistines to conquer them. After forty years of Philistine oppression, the Lord raises up Samson to lead the Israelites against the Philistines. When Samson's Philistine wife is given to another man, Samson ties torches to the tails of foxes and lets them run loose, burning down the Philistines' fields. When the Philistines retaliate by killing his wife, Samson slaughters one thousand Philistines with the jawbone of a donkey. As leader of the Israelites, Samson is a force to be reckoned with—for now.

(Needed: Riddle book and prizes [optional])

Hold a riddle contest. To give kids an idea of what you're looking for, you might read some riddles from a riddle book. Then challenge kids to take turns asking riddles. If you wish, award prizes for riddles that no one is able to solve. Afterward, explain that Samson started his "career" with a riddle.

DATE I USED THIS SESSION _____ GROUP I USED IT WITH _____

NOTES FOR NEXT TIME _____

_____

_____

1. From what you can tell in Judges 13, what kind of parents do you think Samson's mom and dad were? (They were concerned enough about doing the right thing that they asked the angel for specific instructions on what to do to bring up Samson correctly.)

2. What hopes do you suppose they had for Samson? (They had the promise that Samson would deliver the Israelites. Perhaps they expected that he would be well respected, a good and honorable man, strong, and famous.)

3. What hopes do you think your parents have for you? How do you feel about those hopes? Why?

4. What things about Samson do you think might have made his parents proud? (Perhaps his strength and the fact that the Spirit of the Lord used him.)

5. What things about Samson do you think might have disappointed his parents? (Perhaps his marrying a Philistine woman [14:3], his short temper, and his tendency to get into trouble.)

6. Do you think it was OK for Samson to marry a pagan Philistine woman? Why or why not? (God had clearly told the Israelites not to intermarry with the surrounding idolatrous peoples [Deuteronomy 7:3], so Samson should not have done so. However, God used Samson's moral weakness for His own purposes, knowing that it would lead to a conflict with the Philistines [Judges 14:4].) **What are some other situations in which God can use people's weaknesses to accomplish His purposes?**

7. Based on Judges 14 and 15, how would you describe Samson's personality? (Perhaps self-confident, short-tempered, fearless, and impulsive.) **Why do you think the Lord chose such a man to lead His people?**

8. Who would you say was to blame for what happened as a result of Samson's wedding riddle? Why?

9. If Samson were applying to become the next judge of

Israel, what kinds of things might be on his resumé? If you were on a search committee responsible for finding the next judge of Israel, what would you think of Samson as a candidate?

10. **If Samson's story ended at Judges 15, what would you predict for Samson's future? Why?** (Perhaps that he'd wipe out the Philistines. Perhaps that he'd get into more "women trouble." Perhaps that he'd become a national hero. Perhaps that his temper would get him into serious trouble.)

Hand out copies of the reproducible sheet, "Great Expectations." Give group members a few minutes to look up the passages and make the correct matches on the first part of the sheet. (The answers are as follows: [1] God commanded the Israelites not to take revenge; c. [2] God commanded the Israelites not to intermarry with their idolatrous neighbors; a. [3] God commanded Nazirites not to touch a dead body; b.) Then give group members an opportunity to complete the rest of the sheet on their own. When everyone is finished, say: **God specially chose Samson and gave Samson extraordinary strength to do His work, even though Samson didn't live up to all God asked of him. In what ways does God work through you? What happens to God's work if you don't live up to all God asks of you? What might happen to you?** Explain that the next session shows what happened to Samson as a result of his disobedience.

Great EXPECTATIONS

Samson was a great hero, right? Well, maybe he wasn't quite the role model he could have been. Look up each passage listed on the left, jot down a quick summary of God's command, and then match it with Samson's actual action (listed on the right).

____ 1. Leviticus 19:18

____ 2. Deuteronomy 7:3

____ 3. Numbers 6:6

a. Married a Philistine woman
(Judges 14:2)

b. Scooped honey out of a dead lion
(Judges 14:8, 9)

c. Took revenge on the Philistines
(Judges 15:3-5, 7)

How do you measure up to God's expectations in these areas? Fill in the illustrations below to represent your strength in each area.

Keeping a promise or vow

Not letting sexual temptation lead me astray

Resisting the urge to get even

JUDGES 16

I've Got a Secret

After being betrayed by Delilah, Samson loses his strength and is captured by the Philistines. During a Philistine temple celebration, Samson, with one last surge of strength, pulls down the temple pillars, killing himself and many Philistines. After Samson's death, Israel descends again into sin. A Levite, traveling with his concubine in Gibeah, is taken in by an old man. The men of Gibeah (who were Benjamites) surround the man's house, demanding sex with the Levite. Instead, the Levite sends out his concubine. The men of the city rape the concubine and then dump her body. As a "moral wake-up call," the Levite cuts up the concubine's body into twelve pieces and sends one to each tribe of Israel. In response, the other tribes declare war on the Benjamites. All but six hundred Benjamites are killed. After the war, the Lord supplies wives for the Benjamites, and the tribe is restored.

Hand out copies of the reproducible sheet, "Dear Abbai." Let kids work in pairs to respond to the letter. After a few minutes, ask volunteers to share their responses. Then ask: **How would you describe this guy's relationship? How would you describe this guy? How would you describe his girlfriend?** Afterward, explain that Samson had a relationship similar to the one described in the letter to "Dear Abbai."

DATE I USED THIS SESSION _____ GROUP I USED IT WITH _____

NOTES FOR NEXT TIME _____

_____

_____

1. Tell us about the worst haircut you ever received. What was it like? How did you feel?

2. If you had been an Israelite during the time of Samson, how might you have felt about a judge who had such a weakness for women? Why?

3. If you had been in Samson's place, how do you think you would have responded to Delilah's repeated requests to know the secret of your strength (16:6-16)? Why?

4. How would you describe Delilah? (She seems to have been greedy for the reward money the Philistines offered. She also seems manipulative because of the way she cried about how Samson didn't love her. She was smart and wily enough to wrap Samson around her little finger.)

5. Why do you suppose Samson told Delilah about his hair after she had betrayed him three times already (6:17)? (Perhaps he really loved her and couldn't stand having her think he didn't. Perhaps he just got tired of her nagging. Perhaps he had gotten overconfident and didn't think he'd ever really lose his strength.)

6. Do you think Samson deserved what he got? See Judges 16:18-22. **Why or why not?** (Some may argue that Samson deserved what he got because he was just plain stupid to give in to Delilah, or because he'd done all kinds of immoral things and didn't seem to care about his vow. Others may feel that his punishment seemed worse than his sin.)

7. Why do you think Samson got his strength back at the end of this story (16:29, 30)? (Judges 16:22 may be indicating that as Samson's hair grew, so did his strength. When Samson prayed to God [16:28], God granted him a final victory.)

8. In what ways do you think Samson changed after his capture? (Instead of looking to save himself, he was content to die with the enemy. He prayed to God to help him achieve his final victory. But he still seems to have been motivated by revenge.)

9. Would you say this story has a "happy" ending for Samson? Explain. (In one sense, the ending is not happy at all because Samson died a blind, imprisoned man. On the other hand, the fact that at the end of his life Samson killed more Philistines than he ever had before brings some sense of vindication. And his turning to God at the end of his life shows that something good came out of his humiliation.)

10. If you were to sum up Samson's life in three or four words, what words would you use?

11. How do you suppose Samson was most remembered by the Israelites—as the blind man hitched to the grindstone or as the champion who killed thousands of Philistines? Why? How do you think of him? Why?

12. Do you think people today get a "second chance" to do God's work even if they've really blown it? Explain. (While it's not wise to throw your life away, counting on a second chance to save you at the very end, God does welcome us whenever we turn to Him to ask Him to make our lives something He can be proud of.)

Have group members use the back of the reproducible sheets for a writing assignment. Say: **At the beginning of this session, we read a letter to Dear Abbai. Now you have a chance to *write* a letter—not to Dear Abbai, but to God. No one will see this letter except you and God. Take some time to think about areas in which you need a second chance—maybe because you've given in to a certain temptation, or because you haven't done something you know you should do. Write to God about it. Express to Him what you'd like to see when you look back at the end of your life. Then live to make it happen.**

Dear Abbai

Dear Abbai,

My dad started a fried-chicken restaurant called "Colonel Sam's." He uses a secret ingredient that makes his chicken the greatest. But my problem is with my girlfriend. She's a great-looking girl, and I don't want to lose her, but she keeps nagging me to tell her the secret ingredient in my dad's deep-fry batter.

I didn't really want to tell her, but she kept after me. So I finally said that one of my dad's eleven different herbs and spices is dandelion leaves soaked in garlic juice. (It's not true, by the way.) The very next day, my dad's chief competitor—who is located right across the street—starts advertising his chicken as containing that very ingredient. (It didn't attract much new business, though, as I might have told him.) You would have thought that that would be the end of it, but no, my girlfriend came crying to me for my dad's real secret ingredient. So finally I told her that my dad adds lemon juice to the cooking oil. And can you believe it, the next day my dad's competitor starts putting lemon juice in his cooking oil!

The situation went on and on like this, with my girlfriend nagging me and then telling the guy across the street what I told her. But now she says I've made a fool of her too often, and she won't believe that I love her unless I tell her what my dad's real secret ingredient is. Should I tell her, Abbai?

Sincerely,

Colonel Sam's Son

Dear Colonel Sam's Son,

RUTH 1

Where You Go, I Will Follow

Famine has struck Israel, so a man named Elimelech, with his wife, Naomi, and two sons, goes to Moab in search of greener pastures. While they are there, the two sons marry Moabite women. Eventually, all three men die. When Naomi hears that the famine in Israel is over, she returns home. One daughter-in-law stays in Moab, but the other, Ruth, pledges her faithfulness to Naomi and to Naomi's God and goes to Bethlehem with Naomi.

Hand out copies of the reproducible sheet, "What's in a Name?" Challenge group members to match the names with their correct meanings. (The names are taken from *4,000 Names for Your Baby* [Dell].). The correct answers are as follows: (1) d; (2) k; (3) m; (4) e; (5) a; (6) i; (7) n; (8) f; (9) b; (10) l; (11) j; (12) h; (13) c; (14) g. Afterward, explain that the subject of this session's study is a woman who changed her name to reflect the way she felt she and her life had changed. Instruct group members to save the reproducible sheets for use later in the session.

DATE I USED THIS SESSION _____ GROUP I USED IT WITH _____

NOTES FOR NEXT TIME _____

_____

_____

1. What does your name mean? If you don't know, what *should* it mean?

2. The story of Ruth is set during the period of the judges (1:1). What was the spiritual condition of Israel during this period? (There was a lot of idol worship and other forms of wickedness among the Israelites during the period of the judges.)

3. The name "Bethlehem" means "house of bread." How do you think that fits in with this story? (It's ironic at first, because there is no food—there's a famine. But by the end of the chapter, the name is fitting because the famine ends and harvest begins. The name also hints at the ending of the Book of Ruth—namely, that David, and later Jesus, will be born.)

4. If you were writing a novel based on the story of Ruth, how would you describe the character of Naomi? (Tired, bitter, discouraged, someone who could inspire great love in her daughter-in-law, unselfish in wanting the best for her daughters-in-law.) How would you describe the character of Ruth? (Loyal, willing to take a risk, affectionate.)

5. If you had been in the same situation, do you think you would have made the choice that Ruth made or the one that Orpah made (1:14-17)? Why? (Orpah's choice is certainly understandable. She should in no way be seen as a "deserter." She had no future in Bethlehem, and she may have had a very appropriate loyalty to her own family in Moab. Ruth's choice is the more adventurous of the two. Her own words suggest that through her relationship with Naomi, she has come to know something of the true God, whom she now is committed to follow [1:16, 17].)

6. What role would you say God plays in this chapter of Ruth? (God is by no means a minor character. Although Naomi accuses Him of turning against her [1:13, 20, 21], actually it was Naomi's family who had been unfaithful by abandoning their homeland—part of God's provision for them—and marrying their sons to pagan women. God demonstrates His faithfulness in bringing prosperity back to Bethlehem [1:6].)

7. **What contrasts do you see between the beginning of this chapter and the end of it?** (At the beginning, Naomi has a husband and sons, but the land has famine. At the end of the chapter, Naomi considers herself "empty" [1:21], but the land is again full.)

8. **Is there anyone in your life that you would stick with no matter what, as Ruth stayed with Naomi? If so, who? Explain.**

9. **Who do you know that you think would stick with you no matter what? Explain.**

10. **Do you think God had abandoned Naomi** (1:21)? **Explain.** (Naomi certainly thought so. But the rest of the Book of Ruth clearly shows that God has plans for great blessings for Naomi, and also, through Ruth, for all of Israel [because of the birth of the future King David] and all of the world [because of the birth of Jesus, a descendant of Ruth and of David].)

11. **How do you usually respond when things go badly for you?**

12. **When have you felt God's presence as One who sticks with you through good times and bad?**

Have kids form small groups. Instruct group members to refer again to the reproducible sheet, "What's in a Name?" Make sure group members have the correct answers to the matching activity. Say: **In the story of Ruth, names had very significant meanings. In fact, Naomi even changed her name because she thought it was no longer appropriate. Look at the list of names and meanings on your sheet. Choose a name for each person in your small group based on the name's meaning. Notice that the first name of each pair is a girl's name and the second name is a guy's name.** Have group members take turns telling each other which name they chose for each person and why.

WHAT'S IN A *Name*?

Match the following names with their meanings.

_____	1. Alexandra/Alexander	a. industrious
_____	2. Belle/Kyle	b. strong
_____	3. Cara/Darren	c. wisdom
_____	4. Christine/Chris	d. helpful
_____	5. Emily/Emil	e. a Christian
_____	6. Hillary/Tate	f. fair, just
_____	7. Irene/Jeffrey	g. lively, full of life
_____	8. Justine/Justin	h. musical
_____	9. Megan/Brian	i. cheerful
_____	10. Monica/Eldridge	j. loving, kind
_____	11. Pamela/Kevin	k. beautiful or handsome
_____	12. Sheila/Alan	l. advisor
_____	13. Sophia/Clark	m. good friend
_____	14. Vivian/Vivien	n. peaceful

RUTH 2–4

Ruthless No More

Ruth and Naomi have returned to Bethlehem, but as women in the Israelite society, they have no means of providing for themselves. So Ruth goes out to pick up the grain that the harvesters miss. Providentially, she finds herself in contact with Boaz, a relative who, by Old Testament law, has the opportunity to buy Naomi's land, marry Ruth, and so maintain Naomi's family line. Naomi conceives a plan in which Ruth approaches Boaz at night to ask him to act on her behalf. Boaz does; he and Ruth marry. Their son is the grandfather of King David—and an ancestor of Jesus Christ.

To help kids get a sense of the drama in the Book of Ruth, have them form three groups. Assign each group one of the chapters for this session. Let the groups spend a few minutes identifying the different speaking parts in their chapters; then have each group read aloud its chapter in readers' theater style, with different people reading what is said by different characters. Chapters 2 and 3 require at least four readers (Ruth, Naomi, Boaz, and narrator); Chapter 4 requires at least three readers (Boaz, the other kinsman, and narrator). Additional group members may play the roles of field workers, women of the community, and elders at the gate. If you have a small group, combine the chapters.

DATE I USED THIS SESSION _____ GROUP I USED IT WITH _____

NOTES FOR NEXT TIME _____

_____

_____

Q&A

1. What's the most daring thing you've ever done? Why did you do it?

2. Based on the information in Ruth 2–4, what kind of person would you say Ruth was? Give examples. (She was a hard worker [2:7], humble and grateful [2:13], and obedient to her mother-in-law [3:5, 6]. She was not looking for the richest, youngest man she could find [3:10]. She had the courage to risk her reputation for what she knew was right [3:14].) **What kind of person would you say Naomi was? Give examples.** (She was grateful for what the Lord was doing through Boaz [2:20]. She had enough common sense to know the risks Ruth was facing [2:22], but she had the cleverness to come up with a daring plan [3:3, 4]. She was concerned for Ruth's future [3:1]; as a result, she received new hope and a bright future herself [4:14, 15].)

3. What kind of person would you say Boaz was? Give examples. (He was a "man of standing" [2:1]—of good reputation and some prominence in the community. He was wealthy enough to have fields and employees [2:5]. He was generous and considerate [2:8, 9, 14-16]. He was a man of his word [3:18].)

4. In what ways was Boaz, the "kinsman-redeemer," like a "preview" of Christ, our Redeemer? (Just as Boaz bought Naomi's land to preserve it in the family line, so too Christ bought us back from sin to put us in God's family.)

5. In Ruth 4:17, why do you think the women said, "Naomi has a son"? (Although the child Naomi held was Ruth's son, he represented for Naomi a new beginning, a new family, someone to love her and provide for her in her old age. No longer "empty" [1:21], Naomi's arms and life were now full.)

6. In what ways did Naomi take the initiative in improving her situation? (Knowing that Old Testament laws made it possible for Boaz, a relative, to buy her land and marry Ruth, Naomi instructed Ruth to stay near him [2:22]. Then she devised a bold plan to, in effect, ask Boaz to marry Ruth [3:3, 4].)

7. **In what ways did Ruth take the initiative in improving her situation?** (She took responsibility for getting food for herself and Naomi [2:2], and acted on Naomi's daring plan [3:5-15].)

8. **What can you do to take the initiative in developing your relationship with God?**

9. **Why do you suppose the story of Ruth and Naomi was important to the Old Testament people of Israel?** (It told of God's faithfulness, not just to Naomi and Ruth, but to the whole nation, in establishing the line that led to King David [4:17-22].)

10. **Why is this story important to us today?** (David was not the only king that came from Ruth's descendants; Jesus did too [Matthew 1:1-17].)

11. **How do you see God acting in your life to bring about His good plans?**

Hand out copies of the reproducible sheet, "On the Road Again." Point out the different landmarks that parallel Ruth's life. Then let kids reflect silently on where they are in their own faith journeys. Have them mark where they see themselves on their maps. When they're finished, have them form small groups to share with each other where they are in their faith journeys and what they see God doing in their lives.

ON THE ROAD AGAIN

Ruth followed a long road from Moab to becoming part of God's plan for the salvation of the world. God has a plan for you too. Where do you see yourself on this map? After you've identified your "location," draw the road sign ("Under Construction," "Proceed with Caution," "Yield," etc.) that best sums up your relationship with God right now.

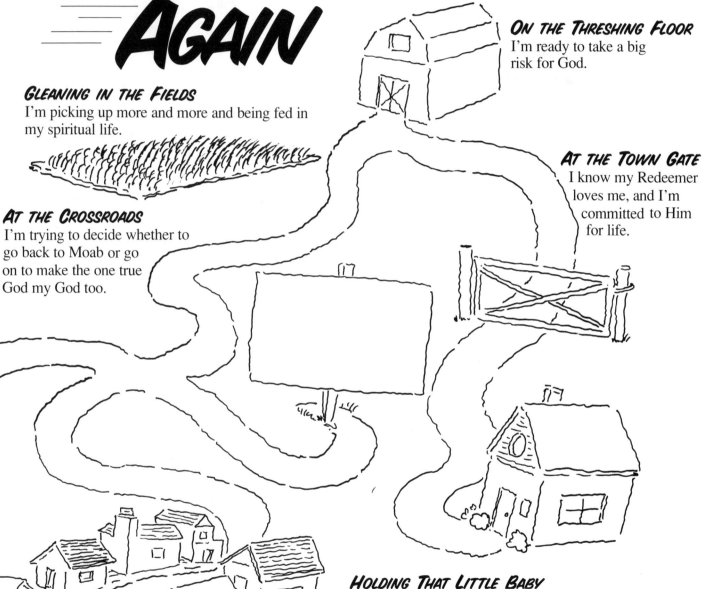

ON THE THRESHING FLOOR
I'm ready to take a big risk for God.

GLEANING IN THE FIELDS
I'm picking up more and more and being fed in my spiritual life.

AT THE TOWN GATE
I know my Redeemer loves me, and I'm committed to Him for life.

AT THE CROSSROADS
I'm trying to decide whether to go back to Moab or go on to make the one true God my God too.

HOLDING THAT LITTLE BABY
I can already see some of the good things God has brought to life in my life. These things include the following:

_____

_____

_____

_____

MOAB
I'm hanging out with people who don't know God, and I guess I don't really know Him either.

I SAMUEL 1–2

Let's Make a Deal

OVERVIEW

Israel is still under the rule of the judges, a period marked by rampant wickedness on the part of the Israelites. Hannah, the wife of Elkanah, is barren—she cannot have children. Her grief over her condition is compounded by her husband's other wife, who taunts Hannah. Hannah pleads with God to give her a son. Hannah vows that if God will give her a son, she will give that son back to God for His service. God gives Hannah a son, who is called Samuel. True to her word, Hannah "gives" Samuel to God by taking him to the sanctuary when he is still very young to live with Eli. Hannah then prays a song of thanksgiving and praise to God. At the Lord's house, Eli's sons are committing wicked deeds and abusing their priestly privileges. The wickedness of Eli's sons is contrasted with Samuel's favorable position in the eyes of the Lord. Because of the wickedness of Eli's sons, a man of God prophesies against the house of Eli.

OPENING ACT

Hand out copies of the reproducible sheet, "Whose Shoes?" Let kids work in pairs to complete the sheet. When everyone is finished, ask volunteers to share their responses. Afterward, explain that one of the worst situations for a woman in the Old Testament Israelite culture was not being able to have children. Lead in to the study of Hannah in I Samuel 1–2.

DATE I USED THIS SESSION _____ GROUP I USED IT WITH _____

NOTES FOR NEXT TIME _____

_____

_____

1. What does the story of Hannah—which includes a barren woman, a loving husband, a taunting rival who is able to have kids, and a miraculous intervention from God—remind you of? See Genesis 16 and 21.

2. In the Old Testament Israelite society, the worth of a woman primarily depended on her ability to bear children. With this in mind, how do you think Hannah might have responded to her husband's questions in I Samuel 1:8? Explain.

3. What might be some modern-day equivalents to Hannah's situation? (Unemployment, disability or illness, broken relationships, etc.)

4. Why do you think God sometimes allows us to experience pain, suffering and grief, as Hannah did because of her inability to have children (1:6-8)? (Sometimes God uses trying circumstances to help us rely on Him.) **Have you ever experienced pain, suffering, or grief that eventually brought you closer to God? If so, what happened?**

5. Do you think that the deal Hannah struck with God was fair (1:11)? Why or why not? Some people might ask, "Why have a son if you're just going to give him back to God?" How would you respond?

6. Have you ever tried to make a deal with God? If so, what did you request from Him? What did you offer in return? What happened?

7. Why do you think Eli assumed that Hannah was drunk (1:12-14)? (Perhaps he hadn't seen anyone pray as fervently as she did. Perhaps because of Israel's wicked state at this time, he was used to drunk people coming in to the temple.)

8. How do you think Hannah felt after sharing her situation with Eli (1:15-18)? Why? Is there anyone with whom you feel comfortable sharing your spiritual concerns? If so, who is it? Why are you comfortable with this person?

9. How do you think Hannah felt when the time came for her to take Samuel to the temple and leave him there for good? Why?

10. Which of the Lord's attributes and works mentioned in Hannah's prayer (2:1-10) means the most to you? Why? Have you ever written a prayer like this to God? If so, what caused you to do it? If not, why not?

11. The story of Eli's sons in I Samuel 2:12-25 seems similar to the story of Aaron's sons in Leviticus 10. Why do you think these priests of Israel had such problems with their sons?

12. How do you think Eli felt when the man of God prophesied against Eli's house (2:27-36)? Why?

(Needed: Chalkboard and chalk or newsprint and marker)

Say: **God remembered Hannah and gave her a very special gift. She also remembered to keep her part of the deal that she had made with God. Take a moment to think of a good gift God sent your way during a tough time in your life.** Write the following paraphrase of I Samuel 1:27, 28 on the board: "I prayed for _____, and the Lord has granted me what I asked of Him. So now I give _____ back to the Lord." Instruct group members to copy the statement on the back of their reproducible sheets, filling in the blanks according to their personal situation. Encourage group members to keep these sheets handy as a reminder of their gifts from and to God.

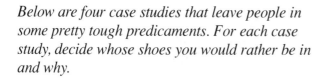

Below are four case studies that leave people in some pretty tough predicaments. For each case study, decide whose shoes you would rather be in and why.

Johann and Lin

Johann and Lin have dated all through high school and are now seniors. They've both recently been offered scholarships. Johann's offer is from a local university where most of his friends will be going. Lin's offer is from a university on the other side of the country, at least a thousand miles away. If they both accept the scholarships, in all likelihood, they will no longer be able to carry on a serious relationship. Either could probably get a job in the same town where the other is going to school; then they could still date. But one would lose a valuable scholarship and give up a chance for a career. Whose shoes would you rather be in? Why?

_____

_____

_____

_____

Linnea and Juwan

Linnea turned sixteen last week, but her parents won't let her get her driver's license until she's seventeen. Juwan also turned sixteen last week, but his parents won't let him get his driver's license until he raises his grade point average from a 2.0 to a 2.5. Whose shoes would you rather be in? Why?

_____

_____

_____

_____

Reggie and Frank

Reggie is a varsity athlete in three sports. He works out all of the time and has an incredible body. However, Reggie isn't very bright. Even the simplest of school subjects are a challenge for him. Frank, on the other hand, breezes through even the toughest classes. No test, assignment, or paper is too hard for him. However, sports are completely beyond Frank. He has no coordination whatsoever. He is also naturally flabby. Whose shoes would you rather be in? Why?

_____

_____

_____

_____

Peninnah and Hannah

Peninnah and Hannah are two Israelite women living in Old Testament times. Both are married to the same man. Peninnah is able to have children, but she doesn't have the love of the husband. Hannah is unable to have children, but she has the love of the husband. Whose shoes would you rather be in? Why?

_____

_____

_____

_____

I SAMUEL 3

A Voice in the Night

After Hannah presents Samuel to the Lord, Samuel remains with the priest Eli in the house of the Lord at Shiloh. One night, the Lord calls to Samuel. He tells Samuel of His plans to carry out His punishment of Eli's family for the sins of Eli's sons. Samuel is left with the unenviable task of telling Eli what God had said. Meanwhile, the people of Israel begin to recognize Samuel as a prophet of God.

Have kids form groups of four. Instruct each group to come up with a skit based on the events in I Samuel 3. The skits should not be simply verbatim reenactments of the Bible account; instead, they should be creative paraphrases. For instance, the sequence in which Samuel is awakened several times by God's voice certainly lends itself to a humorous slant. Encourage group members to have fun with their skits. After a few minutes, have each group present its skit.

DATE I USED THIS SESSION _____ GROUP I USED IT WITH _____

NOTES FOR NEXT TIME _____

_____

_____

1. What do you think I Samuel 3:1 means when it says, "In those days the Word of the Lord was rare"? (Perhaps it means that the during the period of the judges, the Lord communicated very little to the Israelites through prophets and revelations.) **Would you say that the Word of the Lord is rare today? Why or why not?**

2. Do you think the Lord speaks personally to people today in the same way He spoke to Samuel? Why or why not?

3. What significance do you see in the fact that the Lord called Samuel by name (3:2-10)? (Perhaps God is indicating a personal relationship with Samuel. Perhaps He is showing intimacy with Samuel.) **Would you say that you're on a "first-name basis" with God? Why or why not? How does that make you feel?**

4. Even though God knew Samuel intimately, I Samuel 3:7 tells us that "Samuel did not yet know the Lord." How could this be? (The Word of the Lord and His revelations were rare in that day. Samuel had not yet had a personal experience with God.) **Do you think it's possible for someone to grow up in the church today and still not *know* the Lord? Explain.**

5. How do you think Samuel felt after being "faked out" three times by God's voice (3:2-8)? (Perhaps he thought Eli was testing him somehow. Perhaps he was getting tired of being awakened.)

6. Why do you think Eli failed to realize sooner that God was speaking to Samuel (3:8)? (Apparently Eli wasn't familiar with God's voice, and apparently there was no unusual tone about it.)

7. How do you think Samuel felt after he realized that it was the Lord who had been speaking to him? (He may have been a little nervous as he waited for the Lord to speak to him again. He may also have been a little embarrassed at not recognizing God's voice on his own. He may have been excited to realize that the Lord was speaking to him directly.)

8. In I Samuel 3, Samuel is referred to as a "boy." Some historians say that he was probably twelve or thirteen years old at this time. **What does this tell us about the way God uses people?** (God is no respecter of age. He can use anyone to accomplish His purposes, no matter how old the person is.)

9. How do you think Samuel felt about having to tell Eli what God had said (3:15)? (He was nervous about it. Perhaps while he was opening the doors of the house of the Lord he was trying to get up enough courage to speak to Eli.) **Why do you think Samuel felt this way?** (Perhaps Eli had become like a father to him, and it hurt him to have to give Eli such dire news.)

10. Do you think we have a similar responsibility today to confront people who are doing wrong? Why or why not?

11. How do you think the people of Israel were able to recognize Samuel as a prophet of the Lord (3:20)? How do you think people today are able to recognize Christians? Do you think you're recognized as a Christian by other people? If so, how? If not, why not?

The reproducible sheet, "If God Asked Me to . . ." asks group members to rank several potential requests from God according to how difficult they would be to obey. After a few minutes, ask volunteers to share their responses. Then remind group members that whatever God calls us to do, He is also ready, willing, and able to help us with. Point out that God gave Samuel the tough assignment of telling Eli about the punishment that would fall on Eli's house—but God also gave Samuel the exact words to use. Likewise, we can count on God's help *anytime* we do His work.

If God Asked Me to . . .

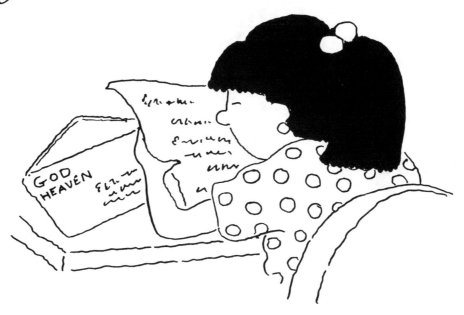

Rank the following potential requests from God according to how difficult they would be to obey (**1 = most difficult; 14 = least difficult**).

_____ *Obey your parents all of the time.*

_____ *Tell one of your friends about Christ.*

_____ *Stand up for someone who's being picked on.*

_____ *Do not cheat on the major test you didn't study for.*

_____ *Go on a mission trip.*

_____ *Go to a Christian college.*

_____ *Volunteer your time at a food pantry or homeless shelter.*

_____ *Talk with your parent(s) about God.*

_____ *Serve on a committee at church.*

_____ *Lead a Bible study.*

_____ *Turn down a date with a really good-looking non-Christian.*

_____ *Teach a children's Sunday school class.*

_____ *Lead a prayer group before school.*

_____ *Sponsor a child from a third-world country.*

I SAMUEL 8

King Lure

After thirty thousand Israelites (including Eli's wicked sons) are killed and the ark of the covenant is captured during a fight with the Philistines, Eli dies from the shock of the news. The ark causes problems for its captors, so the Philistines play "hot potato" with it and eventually return it to Israel. Seventy over-curious Israelites die after peeking inside the ark. The Philistines attack the Israelites during their time of fasting and confession to God at Mizpah. But God protects His people and the Philistines are routed. Israel enjoys several years of relative peace with Samuel as judge. As Samuel grows old, he appoints his sons as judges. They don't rule fairly, so the people complain and demand a king to rule over them—so they can be like neighboring nations. God has Samuel warn the people of the consequences of having a king, but the people still want one. So God obliges their request.

Have kids call out appropriate words to fill in the blanks on the reproducible sheet, "We Want a Blank." Then read the story (which probably won't make sense), using the words kids supplied. See if anyone can guess what the story is really about. Explain that in this session, you'll be looking at a time when the people of Israel really wanted something—but didn't know just what it was they were asking for.

DATE I USED THIS SESSION _____ GROUP I USED IT WITH _____

NOTES FOR NEXT TIME _____

_____

_____

Q&A

Before discussing the passage, get an overview of it by handing out a copy of the reproducible sheet, "We Want a Blank" to each group member. Have kids read through the passage and fill in the blanks with paraphrased words from the text.

1. **Describe a time when you really wanted something. What was it you wanted? Why did you want it? What did you do to try to get it? Did you get it? Why or why not?**

2. **Why did the people of Israel want a king** (8:1-5)? (They said it was because Samuel was getting old and his sons weren't fit to judge them. But later they indicate that they also want to be like the other nations [8:20].)

3. **Why do you think Samuel was displeased with their request** (8:6)? (Perhaps he took it personally because he had been successfully leading the people for many years. It's important to note how Samuel responds to the disappointment—he brings it before the Lord.)

4. **How were the people rejecting God by asking for a king** (8:7-9)? See Deuteronomy 17:14-20. (By asking for a king just like the other nations have, the people were rejecting God as their true King. This is even clearer in I Samuel 10:17-19 and 12:12-15.)

5. **What is a king? How is a king different from a judge?** (The dictionary says a king is "a male monarch [ruler] of a major territorial unit, especially one who inherits his position and rules for life." Judges were men and women that God raised up at various times and in various places to lead the people. Their rule tended to be on a more temporary basis.)

6. **Which of the consequences of having a king do you think would be the hardest to bear** (8:10-18)? **Why?** (Perhaps the loss of children to the king's service or actually becoming his slaves would be hardest to bear. But there would also be taxes—and these would be in addition to the tithe the people were obligated to return to the Lord [Leviticus 27:30-32].)

7. **What additional insight does I Samuel 8:19, 20 add as**

to why the people wanted a king? (Here it's much clearer that they want to be more like their neighboring nations. They especially want someone to lead them in battles. Up to this point, it has been clear that the Lord is the one who delivers His people, not any particular person.)

8. **What are some things people today see their neighbors having that they want for themselves? Why do people want what their neighbors have? Do you think it's wrong to want these things? Why or why not?** (A lot depends on our motives. It's not necessarily wrong to want good things, but if we want them in order to show off, or to look cool, or to be more socially acceptable, then our motives are questionable. Spend some time discussing proper and improper motives for wanting something someone else has. In the same way, the people's request for a king wasn't necessarily bad, but if their motive was to have someone they could rely on instead of God, then it was wrong of them to ask.)

9. **How is God acting like a loving parent in this chapter?** (Three times he tells Samuel to listen to the people. He also wants His children to know the consequences of their behavior. It's often very hard for parents to let their children make choices that will result in pain later.)

10. **Later, the people of Israel got in to all sorts of trouble because of their kings. The nation split in two and many of the kings did all sorts of evil things, eventually resulting in the captivity of the Israelites. If Samuel came back to address the nation *after* the kings messed up, what do you think he'd say?** (He'd certainly be tempted to say, "I told you so." But he'd probably remind the people that it's never too late to return to the Lord.)

Suggest that just as the nation of Israel wanted to be like its neighbors, people today want to be and act like their neighbors. As a group, come up with two top ten lists—the top ten peer pressures teens face today and the top ten ways to battle peer pressure. If time is short, you might have kids split into two groups for this and come together to share their lists.

We Want a Blank

When the leader, _____ grew _____, he/she
a famous leader   *adjective*

_____. So the elders of _____ met their leader at
something people do   *a country*

_____. They said, "You're _____, and your children don't
a place where people meet   *adjective*

_____. Give us a _____ to _____ us,
something people do   *an occupation*   *something a king does*

such as other people have." Upon hearing this, the leader was _____(ed).
a feeling

The leader told them the consequences of their request: "He will take your _____
male relatives

and make them _____. They will _____ in front of
an activity   *verb*

_____. He will take your _____ to be
noun   *female relatives*

_____ and _____. He will take the best of your
an occupation   *another occupation*

_____, _____, and _____ and give them
a possession   *another possession*   *another possession*

to his _____. He will take _____ percent of your
an occupation   *a number*

_____ and give it to his _____. Your _____
a possession   *an occupation*   *something people borrow*

he will take for his own use. He will take _____ percent of your
a number

_____ and you will become his _____. When that day comes,
a possession   *a possession*

you will _____." Even after hearing these dire consequences, the people still
something people do

wanted the leader to honor their request. It was granted. Then the leader told the people to go to

_____.
a place where people go

I SAMUEL 9–15

That's Saul, Folks

Saul goes to Samuel for help in locating some lost donkeys. God prepares Samuel for Saul's visit, because Saul is God's choice to be Israel's first king. After Samuel anoints Saul, Saul successfully fights against the Ammonites. Having anointed a king as the Israelites requested, Samuel gives a farewell speech. Saul makes his first slip as king by disobeying Samuel's instructions in order to appease his impatient soldiers. Then after successfully fighting many enemies, Saul messes up again by not following God's instructions to totally wipe out the Amalekites. As a result, God rejects Saul as king.

Play a game of "Obey the Leader." Call out a series of tasks that must be performed *exactly* as stated. Eliminate kids who mess up. Here are some commands you might use:

• **Turn around** (pause) **clockwise.** Eliminate those who turn counterclockwise.

• **Sit down** (pause) **after taking off one shoe.** Eliminate those who act too quickly.

• **Stand on one foot.**

• **Close your eyes.** Eliminate those who put the other foot down.

Afterward, explain that in this session, King Saul gets in trouble for not obeying God's instructions completely.

DATE I USED THIS SESSION _____ GROUP I USED IT WITH _____

NOTES FOR NEXT TIME _____

_____

_____

1. Skim I Samuel 9–10. **What kind of person would you say Saul was? Explain. Why do you think God chose Saul to be king?** (Besides being physically impressive, Saul demonstrated humility, even shyness—but not when the power of God came upon him. He listened to the advice of his servant. He showed wisdom in keeping silent when some troublemakers didn't support him.)

2. **What do you think Saul's "approval rating" would have been during his early days as king—as evidenced by the incident with the Ammonites** (11:1-11)**?** (It was probably quite high. Note that in verse 6 the Spirit of God came upon Saul in power. This is what brought him victory.)

3. Read I Samuel 13:1-15. **When Samuel first pronounced Saul king, he instructed Saul to wait seven days after arriving in Gilgal for Samuel to come there and offer a sacrifice to God and give him further instructions** (10:8)**. Saul remembered this and waited until the seventh day. But Samuel didn't show up, so Saul offered the sacrifice himself. Then Samuel arrived. What's so bad about that?** (Saul didn't wait long enough. Perhaps God was testing him to see if he really trusted God to defeat the enemy. Saul was obviously influenced by the dwindling size of his army— 1,400 of the 2,000 men he started with had wimped out. Even so, Saul disobeyed God's prophet.)

4. **What was it that God was looking for in a king** (13:14)**?** (An undivided heart—a person who was after God's heart. Later we'll see that David was such a person. David also messed up, but his repentance was always sincere. In I Samuel 13, there's no indication of repentance; instead, Saul tries to justify his actions.)

5. **What are some things you could do to be a person after God's own heart?** (Make getting to know God a priority, spend time with God asking Him to reveal what's on His heart, read His revealed Word, etc.)

6. **When is it hardest for you to trust God for something?** Many of your group members should be able to identify with Saul's impatience.

7. First Samuel 14:47-52 seems to indicate that things turned out OK for Saul after all. Why didn't God take the kingdom away from him like He said He would? (The consequences of Saul's actions don't come until later.)

8. If you were a reporter assigned to cover the story in I Samuel 15, what headline would you use? How would your story open? Summarize the key events you'd cover.

9. What's so terrible about Saul's sin in I Samuel 15? Do you think God was being a bit unreasonable to begin with? (In verse 12, we find Saul setting up a monument to his own honor, not God's. Also, Saul acts as if he had followed the Lord's instructions when he knew full well that he hadn't. He tried to justify his actions. When confronted with his sin, Saul blamed his soldiers, not himself. God's order may seem extreme to us, but He has every right to make extreme demands, even though we can't always understand them.)

10. What are some things people today might do, thinking or saying they're carrying out the Lord's instructions when they're really not? (Going to church for show, giving in order to receive something back, etc.)

Distribute copies of the reproducible sheet, "Pulling Rank." Have kids rank the items in terms of the difficulty they would have in following each one. Afterward, ask:
• **Which command do you think is most unreasonable?**
• **Which would be easiest for you to follow?**
• **Which would be most difficult?**
• **Which do you think God really expects people to do?**
• **How do you feel about God making such requests of people?**

Remind kids that God has a right to demand these things. In fact, He *has* demanded these things in Scripture in one form or another. Point out that even when we mess up, God offers complete forgiveness when we turn to Him in sincere repentance. Challenge kids to consider what it means to be people after God's own heart.

✸ PULLING RANK ✸

Because God is God, He can demand whatever He wants. Here are some things He might "order" people to do. *Put a "1" next to the command that would be hardest for you to obey, a "2" next to the second hardest, and so on.*

____ **Give one tenth of what you own back to God.**

____ **Stop having lustful thoughts.**

____ **Become a missionary.**

____ **Pray continually.**

____ **Love all of your enemies.**

____ **Don't worry about things.**

____ **Save sex for marriage.**

____ **Don't get drunk.**

____ **Always speak the truth.**

____ **Give your whole life to God.**

I SAMUEL 16

The Ruddy Young Man from Bethlehem

After the Lord rejects Saul as king, He instructs Samuel to anoint David, the youngest of Jesse's sons. After being anointed, David is filled with God's power. He's not king yet, but he's clearly God's choice to replace Saul. Soon after, David is called upon to play his harp for Saul and later becomes one of Saul's armor bearers.

(Needed: Seven raw eggs and one hard-boiled egg)

Bring in eight eggs—seven raw and one hard boiled. (If possible, decorate one or two of the raw eggs.) Display the eggs. Have each group member vote for the egg that would be best to eat—but don't let anyone touch the eggs. Ask kids to give reasons why they selected the egg they did. Then let kids gently handle the eggs. See if anyone wants to change his or her vote. Identify the hard-boiled egg and give it to one of the kids who voted for it. Point out that this is a demonstration of the fact that it's not what's on the outside that counts, but what's in the inside. Explain that the eight eggs represent the eight sons of Jesse in I Samuel 16.

DATE I USED THIS SESSION _____ GROUP I USED IT WITH _____

NOTES FOR NEXT TIME _____

_____

_____

1. **Why had God rejected Saul as king (16:1)?** (Saul failed to obey the Lord's instructions on two occasions—first, by not waiting for Samuel to arrive before making a sacrifice to the Lord [13:2-14]; and second, by not totally destroying the Amalekites [15:1-9]. Saul's response when confronted with these sins wasn't sincere.)

2. **What questions do you have about I Samuel 16:1-5?** (Why didn't God simply tell Samuel which of Jesse's sons He had chosen? Why would God tell Samuel to tell a "half-truth" in order to deceive Saul? Why would the elders of Bethlehem wonder if Samuel came in peace? What does it mean that Samuel consecrated Jesse and his sons? [EDITOR'S NOTE: We wish you well as you attempt to answer these questions!])

3. **What does I Samuel 16:6-13 tell us about what's most important to God? What does it mean that God "looks at the heart"?** (People are impressed with outward appearances—even Samuel was when he saw Eliab. God is much more concerned about what our heart is like. That means He cares more about our thoughts, feelings, attitudes, and motives. He cares that we're tender-hearted, not hard-hearted. It's interesting to note that even though God looks at the heart, David is said to be handsome [16:12].)

4. **Do you think most people spend more time thinking about their outward appearance or their heart? Why? How about you?** Have group members suggest ways by which they can tell what's most important to people.

5. **Why wasn't David presented to Samuel in the first place?** (Perhaps his dad thought he couldn't possibly be the one Samuel was looking for. Perhaps someone had to stay behind and watch the sheep, and David was the "low man on the totem pole.")

6. **Read Psalm 23. How do the words of this psalm relate to this incident in David's life?** (It speaks of the Lord being a shepherd, even as David was. It talks about David's head being anointed with oil—a custom of the time that was used to show honor to a guest. It also symbolizes the fact that God chose David. The entire psalm reflects David's "heart" condition.)

7. **How could there possibly be such a thing as an evil spirit from the Lord** (16:14)**?** (Perhaps it means that God allowed an evil spirit to torment Saul. It somehow seems connected to the fact that God had withdrawn His Spirit from Saul. The torment seems to result in severe psychological problems for Saul that come and go the rest of his days.)

8. Have group members write down four sentences about themselves—words that others would use to describe them. Then compare their descriptions to the description of David in I Samuel 16:18. **What does this one verse tell us about David? What does it say about the importance of a good reputation?** (David seems to be a balanced guy—he plays the harp, but is also a brave warrior. He speaks well, but is also good looking. The most important statement is that people recognized David's relationship with the Lord. Because of this reputation, he was invited to serve the king.)

9. **Share a time when someone asked you to do something and you felt honored by the person's request.**

10. **What skills, abilities, and opportunities has God given you? What are you doing to develop your abilities and take advantage of the opportunities in your life?**

Hand out copies of the reproducible sheet, "Outward Appearances." As a group, discuss each case, referring back to David's experience in I Samuel 16. Afterward, ask:
• **What advice would you give each person?**
• **Which character do you think most kids at your school would identify with most? Why? Which person do you think has the most difficult situation? Why?**
• **Why do people worry so much about the way they look?**
• **If someone invented a pill that made people extremely good looking, how much would people pay for it? Would they still take it even if there was a ten-percent risk of getting cancer from it?**
• **What are some things you can do this week to improve the way your heart looks to God?**

Outward APPEARANCES

Write down what lessons each of the following people could learn from David's experience in I Samuel 16:6-13.

SHAWNA is a beautiful, intelligent girl. She's tired of guys wanting to go out with her because she's so good looking. Sometimes she even tries to look bad so that her looks aren't such a big deal to people.

GREG is a late bloomer. He hates the way he looks and is embarrassed by his body. Other guys at school tease him in the locker room. Some days Greg stays home from school just to avoid being laughed at.

JACQUEE thinks she's way too fat. She can't stand to look at herself in the mirror. She decides to exercise three hours a day and go on a very strict diet until she looks thinner.

About a year ago, **MIGUEL** started lifting weights to bulk up. He's made some real gains, and a lot of people have been complimenting him on the way he looks. Now he's hooked. If he misses a workout, he gets really grouchy. He thinks about working out all of the time. He's jealous of other guys who are more muscular than he is.

I SAMUEL 17

Giant Problems

OVERVIEW

The Philistines and Israelites are engaged in battle. Goliath, a giant Philistine, challenges the Israelites to send a man to fight him. The Israelites are terrified. While bringing food to his older brothers, David overhears Goliath's taunts and volunteers to fight Goliath. Saul tries to talk him out of it, but David is confident that God will deliver him. Wearing no armor, David kills Goliath with a slingshot and stone. After David's victory, Saul takes note of Israel's new "hero."

OPENING ACT

(Needed: Tape measure, scale, fifteen-pound object)

Have kids form teams to compete in the following contests:
• Which team can come closest to putting two objects exactly nine feet apart on the floor, without using any measuring device? (Use a tape measure to check the teams' accuracy.)
• Which team can select people or items that will come closest to 125 pounds? (Use a scale to check the teams' accuracy.)
• Which team can throw (or roll) a fifteen-pound object the furthest? (Don't try this indoors.)
Afterward, point out that these measurements all have something to do with Goliath—he stood over nine feet tall, his coat of armor weighed 125 pounds, and his spearhead weighed fifteen pounds.

DATE I USED THIS SESSION _____ GROUP I USED IT WITH _____

NOTES FOR NEXT TIME _____

_____

_____

Q&A

1. If you were making a movie about David and Goliath, who would you cast in the role of Goliath? Who would you cast in the role of David? What would you title your movie? What would it be rated?

2. What does the reaction of Saul and the Israelite soldiers to Goliath's challenge (17:11) **tell you about the Israelites' mindset?** (The fact that they were "dismayed and terrified" seems to indicate that they felt there was no way to defeat Goliath. This shows a lack of trust on their part in God, who had repeatedly delivered His people from their enemies. Note that back in I Samuel 8:20, the people demanded a king to lead them in battle. Looks like their leader was pretty fearful here!)

3. The battle was taking place about fifteen miles from David's hometown. What do we learn about David in I Samuel 16:17-32? (He was obedient to his father. He was perceptive to the needs around him. He was curious. He took Goliath's taunts as an offense against God. He didn't let his oldest brother bully him. He was very courageous.)

4. How do you think David's brothers might have responded when they heard David volunteer to fight Goliath? Explain.

5. How was David prepared for a battle against Goliath (17:34-37)? (He had some experiences as a shepherd in which he battled wild beasts. But more importantly, David recognized that his power came from God alone. He was confident that God would deliver him again.)

6. At first, King Saul refused to allow David to fight Goliath (17:33). Why do you think he changed his mind (17:37)? (Perhaps he finally recognized that the power of the Lord was with David.)

7. In preparation for David's impending battle, King Saul tries to equip David with some armor that David doesn't really need. Has anybody ever tried to make you do something or give you something that they thought was for your good, but really wasn't? If so, what happened?

8. **How do you think David felt as he walked toward his showdown with Goliath?** (Perhaps he was confident of God's power in helping him defeat Goliath. Perhaps he was angry about the things Goliath had been saying. Perhaps he was disappointed that other Israelite warriors hadn't challenged Goliath before.)

9. **What would you say is the most courageous thing you've ever done? How did you feel about it at the time? How do you feel about it now?**

10. **What's the moral of the story of David and Goliath?** (The battle belongs to God. God can use anyone. It's more important to trust in God than in weapons. God is very powerful.)

11. **What immediate impact did David's victory have upon Saul** (17:55-58)**?** (He was curious. David was already in his service and played his harp for Saul, but Saul must not have known him very well, or hadn't taken much notice of him yet.)

(Needed: Concordance or study Bible [optional])

Distribute copies of the reproducible sheet, "Giant Slayers." Let kids work individually to complete the sheet. On it, they are to identify one "giant" in their life—some problem that seems impossible to overcome. If they are uncomfortable naming it, have them use some type of symbol to represent the problem. Then they are to identify five weapons God has given them to fight this giant. If you have time, you might want to have kids actually write five Scripture verses on the "stones." Have a concordance or study Bible on hand to locate verses. Be prepared to share your own struggles against the giants in your life. Have kids share what they've written on the stones. Some might want to share what they've written as their giants, but don't force anyone to do so. Close with a time of prayer, asking God for His help and thanking Him for the way He's delivered His people throughout history.

We all face giant-size problems. Give the giant below a name to indicate some major problem or struggle you're facing right now. It might be a situation at school or at home. It might be some secret sin you've been dealing with. Then label the five stones with weapons God gives us to deal with and defeat the giants in our lives.

I SAMUEL 18–20

That's What Friends Are For

David and Jonathan, Saul's son, become best friends. God grants David great success, and Saul becomes jealous of him. After Saul twice tries to kill him, David runs for his life. His wife, Saul's daughter, helps him escape. David meets with Samuel, and while he's there, Saul can't harm him, though he tries. David and Jonathan hatch a plan to test how much Saul wants to kill David. Saul tries to kill Jonathan when he realizes that Jonathan has sided with David. Convinced of his father's hatred toward David, Jonathan reaffirms his friendship with David and tearfully sends him away in peace.

Have kids form teams. Give each team a copy of the reproducible sheet, "Fast Friends." See which team can successfully complete the sheet first. (The answers are as follows: [1] d [The Sundance Kid]; [2] g [Shirley Feeney]; [3] f [Betty Rubble]; [4] e [David]; [5] c [C3PO]; [6] h [Ethel Mertz]; [7] a [Huck Finn]; [8] j [Milhouse]; [9] b [Woodstock]; [10] i [Louise].) Lead in to a discussion of the qualities that make up a truly great friendship. As you go through the session, see how many of these qualities apply to Jonathan and David.

DATE I USED THIS SESSION _____ GROUP I USED IT WITH _____

NOTES FOR NEXT TIME _____

_____

_____

1. Skim I Samuel 18. **How would you describe Jonathan and David's friendship? How is it like or unlike most friendships you're aware of today? What would it mean for friends today to love each other as they love themselves? Give some examples of "covenants" that friends today might make.**

2. **What emotions does Saul, Jonathan's father, seem to be experiencing in I Samuel 18? What does this tell you about his character, or his heart?** (He seems to be experiencing anger, jealousy, and fear. Verse 10 says that Saul was prophesying after an evil spirit from the Lord came upon him. That might mean he was exhibiting irrational or uncontrolled behavior. Obviously, Saul's heart was full of selfishness.)

3. **Why do you think David kept returning to Saul's palace after Saul had tried to kill him** (18:10, 11)**?**

4. **What do you think Jonathan was risking by speaking well of David to his father** (19:1-7)**?** (Jonathan was the heir to the throne. By supporting David, he was in a sense denying his own claim to be king. He was also risking his dad's anger. In I Samuel 20:33, Saul tries to kill Jonathan.)

5. **Give some examples of things you might need to give up or sacrifice in order to truly be a friend to someone.**

6. **If Saul went to a therapist, what do you suppose the therapist would say?** (Perhaps Saul would be diagnosed as schizophrenic. He has a real problem with anger.)

7. **In just a few sentences, summarize David and Jonathan's plan in I Samuel 20.** (David would skip a few meals in the palace, pretending to be at home. If Saul got angry about it, Jonathan would know that his dad really was out to harm David. It's quite possible that up to this point Jonathan never saw his dad get angry at David. Saul might have told Jonathan that he had no plans to harm David. In this passage, Jonathan lies to his dad. This doesn't necessarily mean that was the "right" thing to do. It's just what he and David planned. This passage, along with many other in the Old Testament, is a story, not a code of ethics.)

8. What factors might have threatened the friendship between David and Jonathan—to the point that Jonathan would fear that David might try to kill him (20:14-17)? (In those days, it was very odd for rivals to the throne to be friends. If Jonathan were dead, David might be able to become king sooner.)

9. What examples of good friendship can you draw out of I Samuel 20? (There are plenty. The key one might be in I Samuel 20:42, which implies that the friendship was grounded in the Lord. The passage also talks about loyalty, following through on promises, sharing tears, showing respect, helping each other out in hard times, etc.)

10. In I Samuel 20:41, 42, Jonathan and David have a tearful parting. When have you felt the most pain over a friendship? How did you deal with the pain?

For a sense of the depth of David and Jonathan's friendship, take a peek ahead at II Samuel 1:26—the words of David after he learns that Jonathan is dead. Some kids might laugh at this and say David and Jonathan must have been gay. Don't tolerate such humor. Instead, help kids focus on what deep friendships are all about. Use the following questions to generate discussion:
• **Some say it's silly to have a "best friend." Would you agree? Why or why not?**
• **Who do you think has a harder time making good friends—guys or girls? Why?**
• **Why are deep friendships so hard to make? Why are they so important?**
• **A lot of people don't have a real close friend. How does it feel to be friendless? What can you do if you feel this way?**

Close the session by giving kids an opportunity to write. Some might want to write a letter or a note to a close friend. Others might want to write a letter to God talking about their own feelings of friendlessness. Others might want to write a poem about friendship. Don't force anyone to share what he or she writes, but give volunteers an opportunity to do so.

FAST F R I E N D S

The left column lists some famous characters. Their famous friends are listed in the right column—but they're a little mixed up. Who can be the first to unscramble the names and match them to their friends?

1. *BUTCH CASSIDY*   a. CHUK NINF _____

2. *LAVERNE DeFAZIO*   b. COOKSTOWD _____

3. *WILMA FLINTSTONE*   c. 3POC _____

4. *JONATHAN, SON OF SAUL* d. HET DUNCESAN IDK_____

5. *R2D2*   e. IDVAD _____

6. *LUCY RICARDO*   f. TETBY BLUBER _____

7. *TOM SAWYER*   g. RISELYH NEEFEY _____

8. *BART SIMPSON*   h. LEETH TERMZ _____

9. *SNOOPY*   i. SOULIE_____

10. *THELMA*   j. SHOELUIM _____

I SAMUEL 24–26

The Fugitive

To escape Saul's wrath, David hides among the Philistines, pretending to be insane. Later, he becomes the leader of a group of discontented soldiers. All the while, David keeps one step ahead of Saul. During Saul's pursuit, David has a chance to kill Saul, but doesn't. He makes an oath not to harm Saul. When Saul discovers that David spared his life, he stops chasing David for a while. During this time, Samuel dies and David marries another wife. Later, Saul resumes his pursuit of David. David has another chance to kill Saul, but doesn't. In return, Saul blesses David, and gives up his pursuit—again.

Before the session, cut apart copies of the reproducible sheet, "A Game of Cat and Mouse" so that each group member has one card. Approximately one third of the group should be cats, one third should be dogs, and one third should be mice. Make sure only one person is the lion. This person should win the game. Have kids follow the rules on the sheet. Afterward, discuss the game. Ask the "lion" how it felt to always win. Then point out that in this session, kids will see that Saul and David were playing a *real* game of cat and mouse. Even though David might have felt like a mouse, he was more like the lion, because God was with him and had no intention of allowing David to be harmed.

DATE I USED THIS SESSION _____ GROUP I USED IT WITH _____

NOTES FOR NEXT TIME _____

_____

_____

1. Have you ever felt like someone was after you—perhaps a school bully or someone you didn't even know? If so, what was it like? What finally happened?

2. Why was Saul chasing David? What had David done wrong? (Saul was jealous of David and feared that David would be the next king. Keep in mind that David has about 600 men [23:13] with him and Saul is pursuing him with 3,000 men.)

3. How do you think this episode affected David physically, psychologically, and spiritually? (Some of David's feelings are described later in the Book of Psalms. It's likely that being hunted like an animal took its toll on David. He was probably tired and scared. Perhaps sometimes he wondered why God would allow him to go through this. The events might also have brought him closer to God, as trials so often do.)

4. Why do you think David refused to kill Saul when he had the chance (24:3-7)**?** (He knew that God had chosen Saul as king. He was willing to wait for God's timing to remove Saul from the throne. You might want to point out that I Samuel 24:3 is a rare indication that even people in the Bible had to take care of certain bodily functions.)

5. Based on the events in I Samuel 24, in what ways would you say David acted more like a true leader than Saul did? (David was brave. He displayed a conscience. He had scruples. He rebuked his own men when they needed it. He depended on God. He showed respect to Saul. He spoke his mind clearly. He used humor [24:14].)

6. Do you think David was convinced of Saul's sincerity (24:16-22)**?** (Obviously not, as he returned to his stronghold, not to Saul's residence. Saul's track record was pretty poor.) **Would you have been? Explain.**

7. How is I Samuel 26 similar to I Samuel 24? (David had another chance to kill Saul. First Samuel 26:10 is key—David continues to wait for God to take care of Saul. David again makes a speech to Saul to prove that he doesn't intend to harm him. In both speeches, David mentions a flea. He's trying to show Saul how foolish he is being in worrying about David. Again Saul calls David "son" and admits that David will ultimately triumph. He leaves David alone again—for a while.)

8. **Saul kept confessing—see I Samuel 15:24 for another example. Do you think he really meant it? What does this tell you about the nature of confession?** (It's hard to say whether he meant it at the moment. God certainly knows if our confession is sincere. Given Saul's track record, his confession didn't seem to have any lasting affect.)

9. **If Saul were president today, what shape would our country be in? How might he be spending his time?** (Things in the country probably would be pretty messed up. He'd probably spend a lot of time worrying about his opponents in the next election.)

10. **Have you ever had an opportunity to "get even" or "settle the score" with somebody who wronged you? Did you act like David, and leave it in God's hands? Or did you take revenge yourself? Why is it sometimes hard to resist getting back at somebody?**

Pretend that you're David, and that you're hiding from Saul. Write down what you might be thinking or feeling. Give kids a few minutes to write; then let them share their thoughts. Compare them with what David actually wrote under similar circumstances. The Book of Psalms is full of examples. You might look at Psalms 3; 11; 13; 35; 64; 142; and 143. **What do these psalms have in common?** (One key thing is that David always trusts God to deal with his enemies. He doesn't take matters into his own hands. He's also very honest with God about how he feels.) **How hard is it to trust God to deal with enemies? Why doesn't God want us to take revenge ourselves?** Read and discuss Romans 12:17-21, which quotes Proverbs 25:21, 22. Have kids think of people they have a hard time loving. **What would it mean to "feed them" or "give them something to drink" this week?**

A Game of CAT AND MOUSE

Cut apart copies of this sheet so that everyone has one card. Distribute the cat, mouse, and dog cards evenly among group members. Give the lion card to only one group member. Don't tell group members what's on the various cards; let them be surprised. They'll think there are more types of animals than there really are. The person who has the lion card won't know that he or she is invincible.

Rules

1. Group members should pair up and keep their identities secret.
2. At your signal, they should show their cards to each other.
3. Here's what happens:
   Cat beats (eats) mouse.
   Dog beats (chases) cat.
   Mouse beats (scares) dog.
   Lion beats everyone.

4. Those who have been beaten must sit out.
5. If there's a tie, both players remain in the game for the next round.
6. Have players pair up again.
7. Keep playing until only one player remains. It should be the lion.

CAT
- You beat the mouse.
- You beat the bird.
- You lose to the dog.
- You lose to the lion.

DOG
- You beat the cat.
- You beat the bird.
- You lose to the mouse.
- You lose to the lion.

MOUSE
- You beat the dog.
- You beat the elephant.
- You lose to the cat.
- You lose to the lion.

LION
- You beat the cat.
- You beat the mouse.
- You beat the dog.
- You lose to the hunter.

The Lie, the Witch, and the War

While hiding among the Philistines in Gath, David and his men raid neighboring enemies of Israel, but lie to the ruler of Gath, convincing him that they've been plundering Israel (or their kin). As the Philistines prepare to attack Israel, Saul seeks guidance from a witch who summons up Samuel from the dead. Samuel tells Saul that he and his sons will die in battle the next day. Meanwhile, David tries to honor Achish's request to join the Philistines in their fight with Israel, but the other Philistine leaders send him away. David and his men find their camp plundered and their wives and children taken hostage by the Amalekites. David and his men rescue their families and defeat the Amalekites. The Philistines defeat Saul's army. During the battle, three of Saul's sons are killed. After being wounded by an arrow, Saul takes his own life.

Ask kids to do an impression of a witch as portrayed in movies. Vote on the best performance. Or you might have kids draw how movies portray witches. Say: **Movies often portray witches comically. In this session, we'll see that Saul consulted a witch for advice. It was no laughing matter.**

DATE I USED THIS SESSION _____ GROUP I USED IT WITH _____

NOTES FOR NEXT TIME _____

_____

_____

1. When was the last time something terrified you? When you're really afraid, what are some things you do to deal with your fear?

2. How did Saul deal with his fear of the Philistines (28:5, 6)? Why didn't it work? (Saul sought out the Lord to help him with his situation. But God didn't answer him. Remember, God's spirit had departed from Saul. Perhaps God knew that Saul's heart was still bent on doing evil. In the same way, our own sinfulness can hinder our relationship with God.)

3. Review God's feelings about sorcery and witchcraft in Leviticus 20:6, 27 and Deuteronomy 18:9-13. Why do you think God detests such practices? (Reliance on such evil practices shows a total lack of trust in God.)

4. What are some inappropriate ways people today try to find out the future? (Horoscopes, Ouija boards, tarot cards, fortune tellers, etc.) Why are people so curious about the future? (People often fear the unknown, so they go to great lengths to find out what's in store for them. That's exactly what Saul is doing in this passage. He knew that consulting a medium was wrong, judging by his past action of banning such practices and by the fact that he disguised himself.)

5. If God hates such practices, why would He allow Samuel's spirit to appear to Saul (28:11-19)? (The whole incident is bizarre. In some ways, the medium seems shocked at Samuel's appearance. Some say it was an evil spirit, not really Samuel. Others say that the medium was a phony, and God baffled her by allowing Samuel to appear. Whatever the case, Samuel speaks the truth. It sounds like something he would have said had he been alive.)

6. Why was God angry at Saul (28:16-19)? (It's interesting to note that even though Samuel seems disturbed with Saul for consulting the medium, the true source of God's anger with Saul is Saul's failure to follow God's earlier instructions regarding the Amalekites. After hearing the news, Saul was probably sorry he had asked!)

7. After Saul heard that he would lose the battle and that he and his sons would die (28:19), **why do you think he returned to fight?** (Perhaps he didn't really believe Samuel. Perhaps he was resigned to his fate. Perhaps he felt some duty to be with his soldiers.)

8. Saul's death is one of the few examples of suicide in the Bible (31:4). **What does that say about Saul's character?** (Saul had been on a downward spiral for some time, so it's not surprising that it would end this way. He had been hurting himself for some time.)

9. **If you had to write Saul's obituary, what would you say?** This is one way to summarize the events of Saul's life. Remind group members that God chose Saul to be the first king of Israel and that he had many military successes early on. But he eventually made some wrong choices and hardened his heart to God.

10. **What steps can you take to make sure your life doesn't end up like Saul's?** (Sincerely repent of wrongdoing, seek God only—even when He doesn't seem to answer, let go of grudges, etc.)

Distribute copies of the reproducible sheet "Bouncing off the Ceiling?" Have group members work individually to complete the sheet. After a few minutes, discuss it. Point out that God turned His back on Saul and didn't respond to his prayers. Your group members may feel that God isn't hearing their prayers sometimes. As a group, discuss some reasons why people feel this way. Be sure to talk about what it means to be called by God's name. If we are called by His name, then we belong to Him. In essence, being a Christian means being called by His name. The only way to enter into that type of relationship is through trusting in the saving work of Jesus Christ. Go through the other items on the sheet as time allows. Encourage group members to talk with you privately if they have questions or concerns about their own relationship with God.

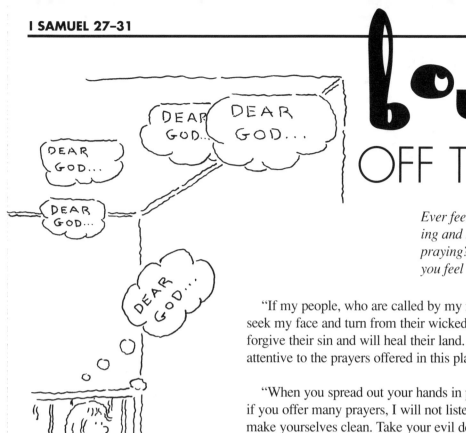

bouncing
OFF THE CEILING?

Ever feel like your prayers are bouncing off the ceiling and not reaching God? Ever feel like it's no use praying? How might the following verses help when you feel like God is nowhere to be found?

"If my people, who are called by my name, will humble themselves and pray and seek my face and turn from their wicked ways, then will I hear from heaven and will forgive their sin and will heal their land. Now my eyes will be open and my ears attentive to the prayers offered in this place" (II Chronicles 7:14, 15).

"When you spread out your hands in prayer, I will hide my eyes from you; even if you offer many prayers, I will not listen. Your hands are full of blood; wash and make yourselves clean. Take your evil deeds out of my sight! Stop doing wrong, learn to do right! Seek justice, encourage the oppressed. Defend the cause of the fatherless, plead the case of the widow" (Isaiah 1:15-17).

"How long, O Lord? Will you forget me forever? How long will you hide your face from me? How long must I wrestle with my thoughts and every day have sorrow in my heart? . . . But I trust in your unfailing love; my heart rejoices in your salvation. I will sing to the Lord, for he has been good to me" (Psalm 13: 1, 2, 5, 6).

Give some reasons why God might not respond to every prayer.

What does it mean to be called by God's name? Are you called by God's name? Explain.

What does it mean to be humble? List some ways in which your own pride could get in the way of your relationship with God.

True repentance involves turning away from wrongdoing. What are some sinful practices you might need to turn from?

After we turn from our wrong ways, God wants us to turn toward right living. This is evidenced by the things we do. What does it mean for you to seek justice and encourage the oppressed?

Other times, God may seem distant because He's trying to teach us something. What can you learn from those times when God seems far off?

II SAMUEL 5–8

A Crown Can Cause Headaches

David finally becomes king. He has already been anointed in front of his family (I Samuel 16:13) and his own tribe of Judah (II Samuel 2:4), but now he is recognized by the entire nation of Israel. After David becomes king, he faces conflicts with outside peoples, with God (after a faithful priest is killed for touching the ark of the covenant when he was only trying to keep it from toppling over), and within his own household. Yet David remains faithful to God and wins many victories.

Cut apart the "secret motive" cards on the reproducible sheet, "Foul Up the Leader." Explain that you think the group needs a king or queen to inspire and motivate everyone else. Appoint or elect someone to be the leader. Hand out the cards to various kids. Then begin a planning session to discuss what kids expect from their new leader. Without being obvious, everyone with secret motives should try to influence the new leader (or the group). This activity should demonstrate that with leadership comes a need for wisdom. People tend to envy the *power* of leadership, but we don't often consider the pressure put on leaders to perform to everyone's expectations.

DATE I USED THIS SESSION _____ GROUP I USED IT WITH _____

NOTES FOR NEXT TIME _____

_____

_____

1. If you were named king or queen of the country, what would be your first three acts? Would you try to make others happy or would you do what *you* wanted? Why?

2. How do you think David felt about becoming king of Israel (5:1-5)? (Any happiness he might have felt was probably quickly subdued by the tasks that faced him as king.)

3. Why do you think the Jebusites were so confident that David could not conquer them (5:6, 7)? See Genesis 10:15, 16. (The Jebusites had occupied Jerusalem for a long time. They may have thought they were invulnerable.)

4. How can you tell when "fighting" for something is the right thing to do (II Samuel 5:7)? For example, why didn't David simply live in a different city? (David ruled with God's authority. While many of our conflicts should be settled by "turning the other cheek," we must "fight" [in some form] anything that threatens us spiritually. David's efforts were rewarded by God, signifying that he had done the right thing.)

5. In addition to his problems *within* Israel, David had *external* problems as well (5:17-25). What can we learn from his approach to handling problems? (David wisely sought God's direction rather than automatically fighting back. That way he was certain to win.)

6. Being a good king also meant seeing to the *spiritual* well-being of the nation. David decided to bring the ark of the covenant to Jerusalem. It was a time of great celebration. But what brought the celebration to a quick end? See II Samuel 6:1-7. Do you think Uzzah's death was warranted? Why or why not? (It seems like a severe penalty for someone with the best of intentions.)

7. Do you think Uzzah's death could have been avoided without the ark being damaged? If so, how? (The warning was clear that anyone who touched the ark would die [Numbers 4:15], so it was designed to be carried on poles [Exodus 25:12-15]. But here it was being transported on a cart—the way the Philistines had carried it. Had things been done the way God instructed, no harm would have come to pass.)

8. David got angry at God, but became afraid of Him as well (II Samuel 6:8-11). **Have you ever gotten angry with God because** *you* **did something wrong and then suffered for your actions? How can you reduce suffering after you commit a sin?** (Being quick to ask forgiveness is the best course of action.)

9. Eventually the ark was safely *carried* to Jerusalem (6:12-19). **But when David got home, he discovered he had family problems (6:16, 20-22). Do you think Michal had a valid complaint? Why or why not?** (While David's enthusiasm was certainly high, it was a result of his genuine worship and celebration to God. Michal seems to have been too proud to rejoice with her husband.) **Does pride ever get in the way of your worship opportunities? If so, in what ways?**

10. God gave David many victories (8:1-14), and eventually David was able rule in peace (7:1). **When things settled down, David wanted to build a temple to house the ark (7:1-17). Why do you think God refused his request?** (God has different assignments for His people. David was to be remembered as the warrior/king. His son, Solomon, would be called on to build the temple.)

11. When David first stepped into the role of king, he faced a lot of problems. **What do you think would have happened if he had given up at that point?** (The peace and prosperity that followed might never have occurred.) **What can we learn from David's example?**

Hand out paper and pencils. Have kids create four categories on their papers: (1) *Internal Conflicts* (problems with Christians); (2) *External Conflicts* (problems with non-Christians); (3) *Problems with God* (personal situations in which kids feel God let them down); (4) *Problems with Friends/Family* (current relationship problems). Explain that if we are to find peace in our lives, we must deal with *all* of these problems. If we don't have the wisdom to do so, God can provide it. We should clearly identify such problems and develop strategies to handle them. Let kids do so in the time that remains.

FOUL UP THE LEADER

You want to get on the leader's good side so you can share in the power he or she will have.

You wanted to be the leader, so you'll do whatever you can (without being obvious) to keep the person from looking good.

You'd like to become best friends with the new leader.

The leader offended a friend of yours years ago. You think that if you can make the person look bad now, you can have revenge for your friend.

You like the new leader, but you have some reservations about his or her ability to lead. You want to ask enough questions to see if he or she knows what he or she is talking about.

You think adult leaders are enough for this group. You wonder, *Why do we need one kid to "lead" the rest of us?*

You know a secret: you once saw the new leader steal some money out of a locker at school. The person doesn't know you saw. But now you don't want this person in charge of the whole youth group budget.

Your new leader seems "clean" enough. But you know for a fact that other members of his or her family hang out in local bars frequently. You can't help but suspect that "the apple hasn't fallen far from the tree."

The new leader recently confided to you that he or she is having some tremendous personal problems. You're concerned that the stress of leadership will be too much for the person.

II SAMUEL 11–12

The Lust Thing on My Mind

After showing great kindness to Jonathan's son, David defeats the Ammonites in battle. Later, however, David has an adulterous affair with Bathsheba, who becomes pregnant. To cover up his sin, David arranges to have Bathsheba's husband killed in battle. David and Bathsheba are then married and have the child. But as a result of their sin, the child dies.

(Needed: Chairs)

Arrange chairs in a circle—one chair for every two players. Divide the group into boy-girl couples. Have the girls sit in the chairs, with one guy directly behind each girl's chair. Guys' hands should be behind their backs. One guy without a partner should stand behind an empty chair. He will wink at one of the girls, who must lunge toward the empty chair. The guy behind her will try to tag her on the shoulder before she gets away. If he does, she must stay with him. If she escapes to the other chair, the guy then becomes the "winker." After a few rounds, introduce the Bible study by pointing out that David was interested in "more than a wink" from Bathsheba.

DATE I USED THIS SESSION _____ GROUP I USED IT WITH _____

NOTES FOR NEXT TIME _____

_____

_____

Q&A

1. While alone in your house, you discover you can see perfectly into your neighbor's window. One of their guests—someone about your age, and of the opposite sex—is *very* attractive. You see that this person is getting ready to take a bath, and is slowly disrobing. Tell the truth. What would you do?

2. This very temptation was too much even for King David—a man "after [God's] own heart" (I Samuel 13:14). Read II Samuel 11:1-5. In this case, where do you think temptation left off and actual sin began? (Perhaps when David didn't divert his eyes. Accidentally seeing a woman bathing wasn't a sin. Even inquiring into her marital status might have been typical of these times, since David already had several wives [5:13]. When David discovered that Bathsheba was married, but then slept with her anyway, his sin became blatant.)

3. The Bible doesn't say, but do you think Bathsheba was a willing participant in this affair? Why or why not?

4. David may have thought he had gotten away with adultery, but Bathsheba got pregnant. She knew it was David's child because she had just had her period (11:4). What do you think David should have done at that point? (Confessing to God probably should have been his first step.) What did he actually do? See II Samuel 11:6-8. Can you think of something you once did that was wrong, but that only got worse as you tried to keep it hidden? If so, what happened?

5. What kind of guy do you think Uriah was? Explain. (He seems to have had more integrity—even when drunk [11:12, 13]—than David did at this time.)

6. What would have been the worst that could have happened if David had publicly confessed his affair? (By law, both parties of an adulterous affair should have been put to death [Leviticus 20:10]. David's position as king may have caused the court to "go easy" on him, but it would still have been very embarrassing.)

7. Why do you think David went to such extreme lengths to cover up his sin (11:14-27)? Can you think of any recent news stories about someone who committed a horrible act just to cover up something that wasn't nearly as bad?

8. With Uriah dead, David and Bathsheba married and had the baby. But God wasn't fooled. Why do you think God revealed David's sin to him in the form of a parable (12:1-6)?

9. Do you think the judgment of God (12:7-14) was fair? Why or why not? (David's own life was spared, but the child was to die—which seems unfair. Yet David would also experience ongoing family turmoil as a consequence.)

10. David begged and fasted for the life of his child. But when the child died anyway, David seemed surprisingly at peace (12:15-23). Do you find his behavior strange? Why or why not? (Prayer is appropriate until God acts. Then, acceptance of His will is the best response.)

11. Some people might suspect that such a major sin—and God's response to it—would cause David to give up on God, or God to give up on David. Do you see any such indication? Explain. (Some of David's most heartfelt writing [such as Psalm 51] was in response to God's forgiveness for this sin. And God blessed the next child of David and Bathsheba—Solomon.) Why do some people think God gives up on them when they do something wrong? (Perhaps they don't understand the depths of God's forgiveness.)

Point out that temptation can topple even the most faithful servants of God if they aren't careful. Read Matthew 5:29, 30. Explain that Jesus' words aren't to be taken literally here, but we should certainly learn to "blind ourselves" to things that tempt us to sin. The reproducible sheet, "Look Away, Look Away," asks kids to consider the things that tempt them and to think of other things to look at when temptation strikes. Close with a prayer for perseverance to stay close to God—not only when things are bad, but also when things are going well.

Look away,

Look away

*An old proverb says, "What you don't know won't hurt you." But when it comes to spiritual things, it might be adapted to **"What you don't see isn't nearly as likely to tempt you."***

Many times temptation seems to begin at the optic nerve. Something we see sets our minds to work, "considering all of the possibilities." And if we aren't careful, before we know it, we've acted on some of those impulses. It would seem that the best thing to do when confronted with a temptation-arousing sight is to stop looking. But that's pretty hard to do—unless we have something else to look at. So for each of the following temptations, think of something else you would expect to see in the same setting—something that would be OK to look at and that would help you divert your eyes long enough to keep from getting drawn into the black hole of temptation. Draw your alternative(s) in the space provided.

	TEMPTING SIGHTS	ALTERNATIVE SIGHT(S) TO FOCUS ON
	1. *Penthouse, Playgirl,* and similar magazines.	
	2. Raunchy movies on cable TV	
	3. Beach babes/hunks	
	4. All-you-can-eat dessert cart	
	5. A peephole into the other locker room	

II SAMUEL 13–18

Revenge, Rebellion, and Remorse

OVERVIEW

Amnon, David's son, rapes his half-sister, Tamar. Tamar's full brother, Absalom, kills Amnon and flees. Even though David makes concessions to allow Absalom to return, Absalom conspires against his father. David leaves Jerusalem for his own safety, and God protects him. Absalom, on the other hand, meets an undignified end. After mourning for his son, David returns to Jerusalem, where he stops another rebellion., After avenging the Gibeonites and battling the Philistines, David—perhaps in an act of pride—orders a census to be taken of the fighting men in Israel. As punishment, God sends a plague that kills seventy thousand Israelites.

OPENING ACT

Have kids sit in a circle for "Backward Storytelling." Start with the end of a story and let each person in turn create the step in the story *prior to* that event. For example, the first person might say, "That's how the flower grew from the crack in the sidewalk." The next person might say, "The rain caused the plant to grow"—and so forth, until you get to the start of the story. Afterward, point out that Amnon's lust began a series of events that ended with the devastation of a family.

DATE I USED THIS SESSION _____ GROUP I USED IT WITH _____

NOTES FOR NEXT TIME _____

_____

_____

Q&A

1. **What's the weirdest crush you or someone you know have ever had?** (Perhaps a teacher, a distant relative, someone from summer camp, etc.)

2. **David had several wives and concubines, so his children weren't a close "family." What kinds of problems might have resulted from a situation like that?** (Among other things, Amnon "fell in love" with his half-sister, Tamar [13:1, 2].)

3. **How did Amnon's feelings lead to sinful actions** (13:3-14)**?** (For one thing, he went to a bad source for advice and then acted on that advice. Feeling a sexual attraction toward someone is natural. But deceit and premeditated rape are horrendous sins.) **Can you think of any other situations in which feelings themselves may not be wrong, but a person's response to those feelings may be sinful?**

4. **It's clear that Amnon felt lust rather than love for Tamar** (13:15)**. Tamar tried to reason with Amnon both before and after the rape, but he wouldn't listen** (13:11-16)**. What do you think you would do if Tamar were your sister and told you what had happened?** Compare group members' responses with Absalom's response in II Samuel 13:22-36.

5. **Absalom ran away and David was distressed. One of David's aides, Joab, went to great lengths to reunite father and son** (13:37–14:33)**. After three years, what would you expect their reunion to be like?** (It certainly wasn't like the prodigal son story. It was two more years before David would even look at Absalom. And Absalom was soon conspiring to take David's throne away from him.)

6. **If you wanted to overthrow one of the most powerful kingdoms in the world—one that was led by a popular military hero—how would you do it?** (Absalom couldn't overpower David, so he tried to manipulate his way to the top by becoming more popular than David [15:1-6]. Absalom had looks going for him [14:25, 26] and tried to use them.)

7. Suppose a handsome young person was about to overthrow the established leadership of our country. Do you think you would (1) boldly side with the new leader; (2) stick with the original leader, even if it meant running away or fighting; (3) wait to see who came to power; (4) openly make fun of and persecute the leader being overthrown; (5) change your loyalty, but try to do it subtly so the original guy didn't find out; (6) become a spy for the first leader; or (7) something else? **Explain.** Point out that all of these responses are described in II Samuel 15–16.

8. Ahithophel, David's master strategist, deserted to Absalom's side. Absalom's biggest mistake was not listening to him (16:15–17:29). Can you think of a time when God seemed to work through either the good advice or the bad advice of someone you know? If so, what happened?

9. Absalom's handsome head, with all of its beautiful hair (14:25, 26), became his downfall. In an ironic set of circumstances, Absalom was left hanging by his head or hair, alive, from an oak tree. Joab took the opportunity to kill him there (18:1-17). What things do people today take pride in that may lead to their eventual downfall if they aren't careful?

10. This session began with Amnon's rape of Tamar and ends with David mourning for a lost son. Do you see a connection between the two events? What can we learn from this series of stories? (The sinful things we do—even the most secret things—may have consequences that are far more devastating than we ever expect. Others may be affected by our sinful actions in ways we can never anticipate.)

The reproducible sheet, "Circle of Influence," challenges group members to try to consider how their own actions might influence others in ways they've never thought about before. After a few minutes, have volunteers share what they have discovered. Close the session in prayer, asking God to help each person be a better influence on others—both those we know are watching, and those we may not be aware of.

CIRCLE OF • INFLUENCE •

By this point in your life, you may be able to see how other people are beginning to influence you. But you might not consider that you influence them as well. When an elderly church member sees you, is he encouraged about the younger generation? When a teacher sees you struggle and persevere to make an "A" in algebra, does she feel that her own children can get past their struggles? Or are you perhaps setting more of a negative example for others? Give the matter some serious thought.

In the illustration below, draw in your features. (That's you in the center.) Then, in the surrounding circle, draw in people other than your peers that you come into regular contact with. Think about family members, teachers, coaches, neighbors, little kids, and especially people you don't usually consider. Fill in their features; then, for each person, try to think of some way you might be influencing that person—either positively or negatively.

I KINGS 3–4

Wise-ing to the Occasion

David chooses his son, Solomon, to succeed him. David gives instructions to Solomon to avenge the wrongs committed by Joab and Shimei. After David's death, Solomon becomes king of Israel. When Adonijah, in a ploy for power, requests that Solomon give him David's concubine as a wife, Solomon has him killed. After fulfilling his father's instructions, Solomon becomes firmly established as king. Early in his reign, Solomon is given a dream by God and is told to ask for whatever he wants. Solomon's top priority is to be a good leader, so he asks for wisdom. God is pleased with his request, and grants it—as well as promising him riches, honor, and fame.

Hand out paper and pencils. Have a contest to see who can wish for the most things. However, if two or more people list the same thing, nobody gets it. Afterward, let kids read their lists, as others cross off any duplications. Declare two winners: the one with the most items left, and the one with the most valuable set of items left. Pay attention to how many kids limit their wishes to physical items. Are any of your kids like Solomon, seeking intangible qualities such as wisdom?

DATE I USED THIS SESSION _____ GROUP I USED IT WITH _____

NOTES FOR NEXT TIME _____

_____

_____

1. On a scale of one to ten—with ten being "extremely important"—how important would you say it is for you to be perceived by others as being smart? Why? (Some young people try very hard to excel. Others don't want to be seen as "brains" or "teacher's pets.")

2. Do you think someone can be smart without being wise? If so, how? (Some people can spout useless facts and figures without having a clue as to how to apply what they know.) **Do you think people can be wise without being smart? If so, how?** (It depends on the definition of "smart." Wisdom involves using God's truth well, and not just having a high IQ, so that we have good sense and know how to act. It also involves a loving reverence for God and obedience to Him.)

3. Be honest. If God said He would give you any single thing you asked for, what would be your request? Why do you think Solomon asked for wisdom (I Kings 3:1-9) instead of something more selfish? (He saw the opportunity for *many* people to benefit from his request. As the leader of the nation, he was concerned for everyone—not just himself.)

4. When was the last time *you* had a strong desire for wisdom? (Some group members may focus on incidents involving passing tests and making good grades, but look for examples in which people needed to make specific practical decisions—which college to attend, what to pursue as a career, how to solve a troublesome problem, and so forth.)

5. God honors our unselfish decisions. He gave Solomon the wisdom he asked for, but also promised him things he didn't ask for—wealth, victory over enemies, and so forth (3:10-15). What are some things you've recently received from God that you didn't ask for or deserve?

6. What does Solomon's decision regarding the two prostitutes tell us about the nature of his wisdom (3:16-28)? (Solomon used his wisdom to address daily, hard-to-solve problems. He put it to use in very practical ways. It involved not only intelligence, but compassion.)

7. What specific kinds of things do you think Solomon needed to know to make the ruling he did regarding the two prostitutes? (The ability to "read" people; awareness of people's needs; parent-child relationships; discernment of truth; etc.)

8. Think of a problem you're currently facing or a decision you're trying to make. How does it compare to the one Solomon faced? If you could tap into God's wisdom, do you think your problem would go away? If not, what might be different about the situation? (We'll always have problems and hard decisions, but wisdom gives us confidence that God is in control and will see us through them.)

9. Do you think most people would rather be respected for their power and wealth (4:20-28) or their wisdom (4:29-34)? Why? What about you? Encourage honesty. Group members know the right answer *should* be "wisdom," but in our culture, power and money get much more attention.

10. If you had the wisdom of Solomon, what would you want to do first? Why?

Point out that many of us wish for wisdom, but don't make much effort to acquire it. God's Word is filled with wise and helpful ways that we can improve ourselves, so a stronger commitment to Bible study is one sure way to become wiser. To help make this point, let group members take the quiz on the reproducible sheet, "Wise Guys." The answers are as follows: (1) I Kings 3:16-27; (2) Daniel 1; (3) Joshua 10:9-15; (4) Acts 9:36-42; (5) Genesis 41:1-40; (6) Exodus 12:21-30; (7) Matthew 17:24-27; (8) Judges 7:15-25; (9) Acts 16:25-34; (10) Esther 5–7. When group members finish, have them focus on any of the answers they missed. Challenge them to begin there as they try to get more involved with Scripture this week. Close with a prayer not just for increased intelligence and common sense, but for the wisdom that only God can provide.

WISE GUYS

The reason you go to school, besides the fact that your parents and the government say you have to, is to learn what your instructors have to teach you. You could just sit at home and read books, but personal instruction and experience is very valuable. The same is true when it comes to spiritual lessons. We need to do more than just "read" the Bible. We need to see what its characters are trying to teach us.

Here's a pop quiz to see how well you've been paying attention. Try to identify the speaker and come up with the circumstances of the quotation. In each case, the person is wisely solving a problem. Match all that you can; then, if you still need help, you can look up the references at the bottom of the page.

Wisdom in Action

1. "Cut the living child in two and give half to one and half to the other."

2. "Please test your servants for ten days: Give us nothing but vegetables to eat and water to drink."

3. "O sun, stand still over Gibeon, O moon, over the valley of Aijalon."

4. "Tabitha, get up."

5. "Now let Pharaoh look for a discerning and wise man and put him in charge of the land of Egypt."

6. "Take a bunch of hyssop, dip it into the blood in the basin and put some of the blood on the top and on both sides of the doorframe."

7. "Take the first fish you catch; open its mouth and you will find a four-drachma coin. Take it and give it to them for my tax and yours."

8. "When I and all who are with me blow our trumpets, then from all around the camp blow yours and shout."

9. "Don't harm yourself! We are all here!"

10. "If it pleases the king . . . let the king, together with Haman, come today to a banquet I have prepared for him."

Speaker and Circumstances

References: *Genesis 41:1-40; Exodus 12:21-30; Joshua 10:9-15; Judges 7:15-25; I Kings 3:16-27; Esther 5–7; Daniel 1; Matthew 17:24-27; Acts 9:36-42; Acts 16:25-34*

I KINGS 10–11

The Marrying Kind

OVERVIEW

As king, Solomon builds a temple for the Lord and a palace for himself. The Queen of Sheba is so overwhelmed by Solomon's wisdom that she gives him many expensive gifts. Not only is Solomon the *wisest* person around, he is also the *richest* king on earth as well. But even with all that God has blessed him with, Solomon has a weakness. He marries hundreds of wives and has hundreds of concubines. These women worship false gods and lead him away from the true God. As a result, Solomon faces several adversaries, and the unity of the kingdom of Israel quickly deteriorates. After Solomon dies, his son, Rehoboam, succeeds him as king.

OPENING ACT

(Needed: Slips of paper prepared according to instructions)

Write several topics (trains, the solar system, spiders, the opposite sex, etc.) on separate slips of paper. Have each person draw a slip and give an impromptu one-minute speech. The goal should be to convey as much wisdom about the topic as possible. Afterward, other group members should be allowed to ask a few questions—either to clarify something the person has said, or to test his or her knowledge. See who appears to be "wisest." Then see how your kids compare to Solomon when he was questioned by the Queen of Sheba.

DATE I USED THIS SESSION _____ GROUP I USED IT WITH _____

NOTES FOR NEXT TIME _____

_____

_____

1. Have you ever been interviewed or interrogated for any reason? If so, what was it like? How well do you handle being questioned by strangers? Why?

2. How would you feel if people came from around the world to hear what you had to say about all kinds of topics? Why? Who is someone whose opinion seems to get a lot of attention these days? Why do you think that is?

3. Have you ever formed an opinion based on hearsay about someone you didn't know, only to have that opinion change after you finally met the person? If so, give some examples. Read I Kings 10:1-7. **What can we learn from this story?** (It's best to get to know people before forming strong opinions about them.)

4. What's noteworthy about the Queen's response to Solomon's wisdom (10:8, 9)? (She saw beyond Solomon himself and gave praise to God, whom she was certain must be responsible for all Solomon had accomplished.)

5. When you see someone who seems to "have it all," what is your first reaction? Why? (Some people may tend to be jealous even before they get to know such a person. Others may try to exploit the relationship for personal gain. Few think to praise God for the blessings of *someone else*.)

6. First Kings 10:10-12 seems to answer the question "What do you get for the man who has everything?" If you'd been the Queen of Sheba, what would you have asked for from Solomon (10:13)? Why do you think Solomon gave the Queen everything she asked for?

7. In addition to his great wisdom, Solomon had all of the riches and fame he could possibly desire. With all of this going for him, can you think of anything that might have caused problems for Solomon? If so, what?

8. If Solomon had such great wisdom, why do you think he allowed himself to get involved with a thousand different women—many of whom were foreigners who worshiped other gods (11:1-8)? Other than the fact that they worshiped other gods, what problems do you think Solomon's many wives and concubines caused him?

9. Do you know of anyone who seemed to move away from God because of romantic entanglements? If so, what happened to the person?

10. What were the results of Solomon's sin? See I Kings 11:9-13. **Do you think the punishment seems to fit the crime? Why or why not?** (Solomon seemed to have had every advantage. God gave him everything he could possibly want. But it still wasn't enough for Solomon.)

11. Suddenly Solomon found himself with enemies (11:14, 23, 26). **How do you think he felt, after such a long reign of uninterrupted peace and prosperity?**

12. When Solomon died, his son Rehoboam succeeded him as king (11:43). But Jereboam's rebellion against Solomon will soon divide the kingdom (11:26-40). **In what ways do you think your life might "come apart" if you don't commit to complete and ongoing obedience to God?**

(Needed: Copies of the list of group members' ideas)

The reproducible sheet, "Compromise Bingo," is designed to help group members admit to the things they've done in the past to impress members of the opposite sex. (Be sensitive to kids who haven't dated.) After the activity, make it clear that the problem with Solomon was not romance, but rather his willingness to abandon his relationship with God to impress the women he loved. Ask: **As you start dating and getting more serious about people of the opposite sex, how can you be absolutely sure that you remain faithful to God?** As group members brainstorm ideas, compile a list. Later, make copies of the list. But beyond handing out copies, challenge group members to commit to the ideas on the list as they begin or continue their dating lives. Close with a prayer for God's ongoing wisdom—especially during romantic times when various temptations can be particularly strong.

COMPROMISE BINGO

Which of these things have you done while relating to a "special" person of the opposite sex?

When confronted by members of the opposite sex, most of us tend to get a little loopy. We do strange things that are not at all like our "normal" behavior. The card below contains several things people do when they fall in love or want to impress someone. Fill in as many spaces as possible, following these instructions:

1. Walk up to anyone and ask about one specific square. If the person admits to the behavior, get his or her initials in that square. If not, go to another person.

2. You may not ask anyone a second question until you've asked everyone a question.

3. You must be completely honest in responding to questions people ask you.

4. Fill as many squares as possible.

5. Have fun.

SAID SOMETHING YOU DIDN'T MEAN IN ORDER TO GET ON THE PERSON'S GOOD SIDE	PICKED UP A PHONE TO CALL, BUT HUNG UP BECAUSE YOU WERE SCARED	ASKED SOMEBODY TO ASK SOMEBODY ABOUT THE AVAILABILITY OF THE PERSON	SKIPPED CHURCH TO SPEND MORE TIME WITH THE PERSON	SAID THAT YOU AGREED WITH SOME RELIGIOUS OPINION OF THE PERSON, EVEN THOUGH YOU DIDN'T
DENIED SOMETHING YOU KNEW TO BE TRUE TO KEEP FROM POSSIBLY OFFENDING THE PERSON	CANCELED A COMMITMENT TO SOMEONE ELSE AT THE LAST MINUTE TO BE WITH THE PERSON	LIED TO YOUR PARENTS ABOUT THE PERSON	BOUGHT THE PERSON A MEAL OR PRESENT THAT WAS WAY OUT OF YOUR PRICE RANGE	SKIPPED SCHOOL TO BE WITH THE PERSON
HELPED THE PERSON CHEAT ON A TEST OR HOMEWORK ASSIGNMENT	LIED TO THE PERSON TO APPEAR MORE COOL THAN YOU REALLY ARE	**FREE SPACE**	STOLEN SOMETHING TO GIVE TO THE PERSON	MADE UP A STORY FOR YOUR BOSS SO YOU COULD GET OFF WORK TO BE WITH THE PERSON
DAYDREAMED ABOUT THE PERSON WHEN YOU SHOULDN'T HAVE	READ *PENTHOUSE, PLAYGIRL,* OR SOME SIMILAR MAGAZINE TO SEE HOW "REAL" MEN OR WOMEN ACT	STARVED OR WORKED YOURSELF MORE THAN YOU SHOULD TO GET IN SHAPE	TOLD THE PERSON YOU LOVED SOMETHING THAT HE OR SHE LIKED, EVEN THOUGH YOU HATED IT	WRITTEN A NOTE TO THE PERSON THAT YOU NEVER SENT
CARVED THE PERSON'S INITIALS IN A TREE OR A PIECE OF PUBLIC PROPERTY	DECLINED AN OFFER TO GO OUT WITH FRIENDS BECAUSE YOU WANTED TO SIT AROUND AND THINK ABOUT THE PERSON	DID SOMETHING REALLY DANGEROUS TO IMPRESS THE PERSON	TOOK UP A COMPLETELY NEW HOBBY OR INTEREST TO BE CLOSE TO THE PERSON	DID WITHOUT SOMETHING YOU REALLY ENJOYED TO KEEP FROM BEING THOUGHT OF AS "WEIRD" BY THE PERSON

I KINGS 17

Edible Miracles

After Solomon's death, the kingdom of Israel splits into two factions: Israel and Judah. Rehoboam, Solomon's son, becomes king of Judah; Jeroboam becomes king of Israel. After Jeroboam dies, the kings who succeed him all do evil in the sight of the Lord. Things in Judah aren't much better. During Rehoboam's reign, the Egyptians attack Jerusalem and carry off the treasures of the palace and temple. Back in Israel, King Ahab (the wickedest king of all) marries Jezebel. God sends the prophet Elijah to tell Ahab that God will stop the rain. While Elijah waits for further instructions, God provides for his needs by sending ravens with food. When Elijah is sent to a widow's home, God miraculously provides food for Elijah, the widow, and her son.

(Needed: Food)

Begin the session with an eating game. You might hold an eat-a-pie-without-using-hands contest. Or you might have kids form pairs to compete to see who can successfully lob grapes or popcorn into each other's mouths from a designated distance. Or you might combine these and other food-related activities for a "Feeding Frenzy Decathlon." Afterward, move from your kids' own strange feeding behavior to Elijah's.

DATE I USED THIS SESSION _____ GROUP I USED IT WITH _____

NOTES FOR NEXT TIME _____

_____

_____

1. What's the strangest thing you've ever eaten? Is there anything you would *never* eat, no matter what? Where's the most unusual place you've ever had a meal?

2. Why do you think God used ravens to take care of Elijah's food needs (17:2-6)? Can you think of a personal example of when God took care of you in an unusual way? If so, what happened?

3. Do you think God still controls things like how much it rains (17:1)? Explain. Do you think every drought or flood is a judgment? Why or why not? (God can certainly control such things, but opinions vary as to how much He chooses to do so for some specific purpose. However, point out that in this case "rain" also symbolizes God's blessing.)

4. God shows Elijah—and us—that He has no shortage of creative ways of taking care of His people (17:7-16). But if you were a parent responsible for your child and had only one meal left, do you think you would give it up under any circumstances? What would you think about a stranger who said, "God wants you to give *me* that food, and then He will take care of you?"

5. If you were Elijah, do you think you could have asked the widow to use the very last of her food to feed you rather than herself and her son? Why? (Elijah had the faith to believe that God would do as He promised. The widow also had faith—and little to lose if Elijah had been wrong. We always need to obey God, even when His instructions seem unusual.)

6. How do you think the widow felt each day when she went to the jar of flour and jug of oil to find that they still hadn't run dry (17:15, 16)? How does God reward faithfulness in similar ways today? (His demonstrations may not be as clear or as direct, but He always honors a person's ongoing faithfulness to Him through peace, provision, and other related blessings.)

7. If God gave you a flour jar and an oil jug that never got empty, no matter how much you used, do you think you would ever doubt His power or His blessing on you? **Explain.** See I Kings 17:17-20. (Both the widow and Elijah seemed to question God when the widow's son died. Similarly, people can see the wonders of God around them every day and still have some doubts that He is in charge of things.)

8. **After questioning God for allowing the widow's son to die** (17:20)**, Elijah asks God to bring the young man back to life** (17:21)**. What does this tell you about Elijah's faith?** (Though his feelings were a bit confused, he still knew that God was supreme. And Elijah acted on what he *knew*, rather than what he *felt*.) **Are you able to maintain your faith even when you don't feel that God is particularly close? If not, why not? If so, how?**

9. **God's response to Elijah's request is the first recorded resurrection in the Bible** (17:22)**. What do you find significant about it?** (This was the son of a poor widow. The woman and her son weren't even from the nation of Israel. Yet they were the ones to whom Elijah had been sent, and the faith they placed in God was not in vain.)

10. **If you were able to act on your faith in God, in spite of your feelings, what is one thing you might need to do right now?** (Perhaps confess a personal sin, confront a friend about a problem, attempt to restore a broken relationship, tell someone about Jesus, etc.) **How could you accumulate enough faith to take action?**

Point out the connection between the widow's willingness to feed Elijah and his subsequent availability when her son needed help. In this case, they were both following God's leading. But we never know when we do a favor for someone else how God might use that incident to change the person's (or our own) life. The reproducible sheet, "Assorted Favors," challenges kids to think of ways to minister to other people on a daily basis—for a week, at least. Encourage kids to follow through on the things they think of. Close in prayer, asking God to make your kids more servant-minded as they become increasingly aware of the possibilities around them.

Assorted Favors

You know you're supposed to do good things for other people. Yet if you're like most people, sometimes you need to be reminded. Spend a few minutes thinking about all of the people you come into contact with on a regular basis—and what favors you might be able to do for them. Then try to plan at least one "daily good deed" during the coming week. Use lines to connect the following ideas or write in some ideas of your own.

Day of the Week	Possible Favors	Possible Recipients
Sunday	Cook or buy dinner for	Family members
	Do work for	Distant relatives
Monday	Write to	Strangers
	Baby-sit or dog-sit for	Friends
Tuesday	Make something for	Teachers
	Send card to	Coaches
Wednesday	Teach something to	Church members
	Send anonymous gift to	Young person
Thursday	Spend time with	Neighbor
	Read to	Shut-in person
Friday	Go on a walk with	New kid in town
	Call up and chat with	Youth leader
Saturday	(You come up with something)	(You come up with somebody)

I KINGS 18

The Showdown

OVERVIEW

Elijah tells King Ahab that God will again send rain to the land after a three-year drought. Elijah arranges a demonstration on top of Mount Carmel at which the priests of Baal will offer sacrifices to their god and Elijah will pray to God. The people of Israel agree to follow the God who responds with fire from heaven. The priests of Baal try all day to get a response and fail. Then Elijah drenches his altar with water. God immediately responds to Elijah's prayer with fire that consumes the offering, the water, and even the stones. The people of Israel praise God—and it begins to rain.

OPENING ACT

Play the "Picnic Game." Say: **We're going on a picnic, and I'm bringing _____.** What you say you will bring depends on your initials. If your name is B̲ob S̲mith, you might bring b̲ean s̲alad, b̲roiled s̲teaks, etc. Ask the next person: **What are you going to bring?** To any answer that doesn't reflect the person's initials, say: **No, you can't bring that.** Then move on to the next person. If kids don't catch on, name something else *you* can bring and try again. Play until kids figure out the secret. Point out that when you know the "trick," the game is easy. In introducing the contest on Mount Carmel, explain that Elijah knew the real God and had no problem, while the priests of Baal had no clue who God was.

DATE I USED THIS SESSION _____ GROUP I USED IT WITH _____

NOTES FOR NEXT TIME _____

_____

_____

1. Have you been part of an organization in which you felt at ease, yet became uncomfortable or embarrassed when you represented that organization in a different setting? If so, why? (For instance, wearing a Scout or band uniform in public rather than in the group can be embarrassing for some people. Trying to profess Christianity at school rather than at church can be embarrassing for others.)

2. As much as we might feel uncomfortable in such situations, we seldom face life-or-death situations. What was Obadiah's fear in I Kings 18:1-15? (Obadiah was a believer who served God faithfully, but secretly. He didn't want to be publicly associated with the "rebel" Elijah.) What might be a similar situation today in which you would feel really uneasy?

3. Elijah had good news for the king, but didn't share it right away. He was more concerned about the spiritual welfare of the people. Why do you think Elijah suggested a "contest" between himself and the prophets of Baal (18:16-24)? (Perhaps to create a public forum in which the people could witness the power of God.)

4. If you were competing alone against 850 opponents, how do you think you would feel? Why? How do you think Elijah felt about competing against the prophets of Baal? (Elijah knew he wasn't alone—he had God on his side. So it's likely that he wasn't very concerned about his opponents. Remember, Elijah was the one who made the challenge in the first place.)

5. Why do you think the people of Israel were so responsive to Elijah's suggestion (18:22-24)? (They had followed Baal a long time, but seemed eager to see some real power from a god—whether Baal or the true Lord.) If you'd been among the people of Israel, who do you think you would have bet on—Elijah or the prophets of Baal? Why? What odds might oddsmakers have given for Elijah to win?

6. Do you think Elijah had *any* doubt that God would come through for him? Explain. See I Kings 18:27. (Elijah probably wouldn't have made fun of the prophets of Baal if he feared that the same thing could happen to him.) **Have you ever been this sure that God would do something you were hoping for? Why or why not?**

7. **How do you think the prophets of Baal felt about their god's refusal to answer them (18:26-29)? How do you think the people of Israel felt about Baal's silence?**

8. **How did Elijah prepare the people of Israel for God's power (18:30-37)? What was significant about his actions?** (He called the people closer. He repaired the altar of God that had been neglected for too long. He set up twelve stones to call attention to the unity of Israel. He doused the altar three times with water to show that God's power was not restricted by physical conditions.)

9. **How do you think the people of Israel felt after seeing a sample of God's enormous power** (18:38-40)? (Perhaps they felt ashamed for following false gods for so long. Note how quick they were to obey Elijah's instructions to kill the prophets of Baal.)

10. **It had taken only a two-sentence prayer for Elijah to summon God's fire from heaven (18:36, 37). But Elijah had to pray seven different times to receive the rain God had promised** (18:41-45). **What is significant about this contrast?** (Even when we know God's will for our lives, we need to pray faithfully to receive it—whether it comes soon or takes a while.)

Hand out copies of the reproducible sheet, "I've Seen Fire & I've Seen Rain." First, let kids consider how God demonstrates both His power and His blessings in their lives. Then have them think of one situation they are currently facing in which they need to experience a similar demonstration of God's power. Let volunteers show their illustrations when they finish. Close by praying for the situations kids have identified. Ask God to give your kids confidence in the fact that He will come through for them—no matter what the circumstances or how outnumbered they are.

I've Seen Fire & I've Seen Rain

You're an outlaw. You've been "on the lam" for three years. Your face appears on Israel's Most Wanted and people are looking for you. The king of the country would like nothing better than to see you dead. You're alone against forces of hundreds or thousands. But you don't mind. You have a secret. You know something they don't know. You know . . . God! At least, that was true for Elijah. Is it true for you as well?

Elijah knew that fire falling from heaven would reveal God's power. Rain falling would demonstrate His blessings. In the illustration below, list the things that help you be sure of God's power (the fire) and that keep you aware of His blessing (the rain). Then, in the main box, draw a situation that you have recently faced (or are likely to face soon) in which you felt (or might feel) outnumbered or overwhelmed.

I KINGS 19

Ah, Look at All the Lonely Prophets

OVERVIEW

Elijah panics when Jezebel threatens his life. But God tends to His weary prophet, first with an angel to take care of his physical needs and then with a personal conversation to ease Elijah's mind. Finally, God provides Elijah with an assistant, Elisha, to prevent Elijah from feeling alone and to have someone ready to follow in his footsteps.

OPENING ACT

(Needed: Candy)

Give ten pieces of candy to each person. Instruct each person to think of something he or she believes most of the other kids have done that he or she hasn't. For instance, one person might suggest "flying on an airplane." At that point, everyone who *has* flown on a plane must give the person a piece of candy. In turn, he or she must give one piece of candy to each person in the group who *hasn't* flown on a plane. Kids should see that when they try to put themselves in a minority, they discover that more people share their experiences than they may think. Afterward, point out that even though Elijah felt alone, God knew of thousands more who were on his side.

DATE I USED THIS SESSION _____ GROUP I USED IT WITH _____

NOTES FOR NEXT TIME _____

_____

_____

1. When was the last time you felt terribly lonely or scared? What were the circumstances? How did you overcome your negative feelings?

2. How would you feel if the First Lady called a press conference to say that you would be dead within twenty-four hours? What would you do?

3. Elijah had already stood up to King Ahab and hundreds of false prophets—and had won. He had seen God send fire from heaven and rain after three years of drought (18:16-46). **So why do you suppose he panicked when Queen Jezebel issued her threat (19:1-3)?** (Everyone goes through periods of doubt, fear, fatigue, feelings of aloneness, physical exhaustion, and so forth. Any of these emotions might have been bothering Elijah. He may also have been experiencing a letdown after a "mountaintop experience.")

4. If you were Elijah, what might be your biggest complaints? Compare group members' responses to Elijah's words in I Kings 19:9, 10. (Elijah felt alone, afraid, and disappointed that his hard work didn't seem to have accomplished much.) **When was the last time you felt the same way?**

5. If you knew God was going to make Himself known to you, would you be more likely to expect Him to come with a rock-shattering wind, an earthquake, a fire, or a gentle whisper (19:11-13)? Why?

6. Why do you think God spoke to Elijah in a whisper? (Perhaps because Elijah already knew the immense power of God and now needed to be aware of God's sensitivity and compassion.)

7. Would you say that Elijah responded well to the voice of God (19:13, 14)? Why or why not? (It doesn't appear so. Even after this special revelation of God, Elijah voiced the same complaints.) **In what ways do people today fail to respond to God?** (Many people are chronic complainers, even though they can see God's good gifts all around them.)

8. Put yourself in Elisha's position. You're out plowing your field one day when some guy comes up to you and throws his cloak around you, designating you to be the next prophet of Israel. How might your response have differed from Elisha's (19:19-21)?

9. Why do you think God called Elisha to service while Elijah was still living? (Certainly Elisha could learn from Elijah. Also, perhaps having an apprentice might have prevented Elijah from feeling so alone.)

10. Do you have someone you can go to for comfort or assurance whenever you feel terribly lonely? If so, in what ways does that person help you?

11. How did God provide for Elijah's physical, emotional, social, and spiritual needs in I Kings 19? How does He provide for such needs for us today?

Point out that many people can do something great for God if it's a "one time only" event. But when it comes to a twenty-four-hours-a-day, seven-days-a-week consistent faith, many of us fall short—even Elijah. Finding a protégé to teach helped change Elijah's depressed mood and restore his hope. Hand out copies of the reproducible sheet, "Ele-Mentor-y, My Dear Watson." Let group members provide words of wisdom for a person who might come to them for advice. After a few minutes, allow volunteers to share what they wrote. Then encourage each person to find a mentor—someone older and wiser to spend time with and learn from. Challenge older or more mature group members to find someone to be a mentor *to*—a younger person who could benefit from their own expertise about life. Close the session in prayer, asking God to be a mentor for *all* of your group members, and to teach them to become more like Him.

ELE-MENTOR-Y,
My Dear Watson

Holmes had Watson; Elijah had Elisha. Some of the best relationships in history have resulted when someone was willing to spend time with another to become his or her mentor (which, according to Webster, is "a trusted counselor or guide"). Just think how your own life might change if you had someone to sit at your feet and learn from the vast experience you've accumulated during your lifetime. Your unparalleled wisdom and expertise could change some other person's life in ways unimaginable. So take a moment to practice for when someone comes to you for advice.

Complete the following sentences as if you're trying to help out a fellow struggler on the road through adolescence. (Remember, the trick is to sound as wise as possible, while still being truthful.)

The three most important things in life are . . .

The three most enjoyable things in life are . . .

If you try really hard, you can probably get along with everyone in life except for . . .

In terms of dating, the three most important things to remember are . . .

When your parents are really, really mad, the one trick that almost always calms them down is . . .

The top three things you should watch out for—the things that can really hurt you if you aren't careful—are . . .

And finally, remember that life is just a _____ because . . .

I KINGS 21–22;
II KINGS 9:30-37

From the Vineyard to the Graveyard

When King Ahab cannot buy the vineyard of a man named Naboth, Queen Jezebel arranges to have Naboth stoned to death. God sends Elijah to prophesy the deaths of Ahab and Jezebel, specifically stating that dogs will lick the blood of Ahab and will devour Jezebel. Later, during a battle, Ahab is shot with an arrow and bleeds to death on his chariot. As the chariot is being cleaned, dogs lick Ahab's blood, thus fulfilling Elijah's prophecy. Sometime later, Jezebel is thrown from a window and killed. Before her body can be buried, dogs devour it, thus fulfilling the other part of Elijah's prophecy.

Hand out copies of the reproducible sheet, "Shades of Green." Give kids a few minutes to complete it; then see which items on the list would cause kids to be most envious. If time permits, let kids put together skits based on some of the situations on the sheet and act out how they might respond. Afterward, discuss why, since many people have everything they truly *need*, we so often get jealous of anyone who has *more*.

DATE I USED THIS SESSION _____ GROUP I USED IT WITH _____

NOTES FOR NEXT TIME _____

_____

_____

1. Is there something you desperately want right now, but see no way of getting? If so, what is it? What do you do when you want something you can't have? (Some people may daydream about it. Others may give up on it and devote time and energy elsewhere.) **How do you feel about people who have the thing that you desire so badly? Why?**

2. **If you were king or president of a nation, do you think there is anything you might want that you couldn't get? If so, what?** Compare group members' responses with King Ahab's desire to own Naboth's vineyard in I Kings 21:1, 2.

3. **Do you possess something that you wouldn't sell at any price? Explain.** (Perhaps a gift from a boyfriend or girlfriend, an item left in a grandparent's will, etc.)

4. **Why do you think Naboth refused to sell his vineyard or make some arrangement with King Ahab** (21:3)? (The land of Israel had been divided by the various tribes and was not to be sold permanently [Leviticus 25:23-28]. Naboth was trying to obey the law of God that Ahab wanted to break.)

5. **When you don't get your way about something, do you tend to respond more like Ahab** (I Kings 21:4) **or Jezebel** (21:5-16)? **Which is preferable? Why?** (Neither sulking nor scheming are good responses to disappointment. It is much better to trust God and get on with one's life.)

6. **Do you know people similar to Ahab and Jezebel— people who are willing to prey on others just because they have the money and power to do so? If so, how do you feel about such people? Why do you think God allows such unfair treatment?** (He doesn't. [See I Kings 21:17-29.] While He may not *immediately* call people into account for their actions, He *will* do so eventually.)

7. **Which do you think would be worse: to be disciplined as soon as you did something wrong or to know that your punishment was sure to take place, but at some unspecified time in the future? Why?** If no one mentions it, point out that Ahab and Jezebel lived the rest of their lives with Elijah's prophecy hanging over them.

8. It was three years before Ahab died (22:1). To anyone looking on, his death would have seemed purely coincidental (22:29-40). Would you agree? Why or why not? (God can control even arrows shot "at random" to accomplish what He said He would do. The "coincidence" is stretched even farther when Ahab's blood is "licked up" by dogs.) **Can you think of a recent "coincidence" in your life that might actually have been God at work? Explain.**

9. Jezebel's death was more deliberate. She had been arrogant, defiant, and wicked her entire life, but her death was quite humiliating (II Kings 9:30-37). She was thrown from a high window, trampled by horses, and eaten by dogs. Why do you think she met with such a disgusting end? (She had led a disgusting life. She never showed remorse for sin, and she had endlessly persecuted God's prophets. People may have questioned why God would allow her to remain queen, but their questions should have been answered when they heard of her death.)

10. Do you think the deaths of Ahab and Jezebel were a direct result of having Naboth killed to get his vineyard—or was there more involved? Explain. (Their greed toward Naboth was simply a symptom of their true character. While that act in itself was heinous, it was simply the "tip of the iceberg" of all of the sins they intentionally committed while they were supposed to be leading God's people.)

Point out that people like Ahab and Jezebel don't become the way they are overnight. They don't start out by having people killed to acquire property. In most cases, such greed and lack of compassion begin with little things and then grow quickly. Have your kids brainstorm ways they can prevent greedy "little things" from taking root. Make a list of their suggestions. Then challenge them to take their own advice and spend a week "weeding out greed" from their lives. For example, they might think of something they've been hoarding and share it with others. Close with prayer, asking God to point out—and help weed out—all of the "little" things that we allow to affect us.

Shades of Green

Jealousy is sometimes called "the green-eyed monster." But some things probably make you more jealous than others. In each of the following situations, determine how "green" you would be. *Check the appropriate response from the following choices:*

- **First-Signs-of-Mold-on-an-Orange Green**—a little bit green, but not too bad
- **Granny Smith Apple Green**—still on the light side, but getting darker
- **Dill Pickle Green**—medium green, inside and out
- **Chameleon Green**—green is your natural color, but you don't always show it
- **The Incredible Hulk Green**—no doubt about it, you're as green as green gets

Situation

You've had your license for months and have been pleading with your parents for a car—any beater of a car. The day your best friend turns sixteen, he or she gets a brand new convertible.

All of your friends make it into a special club or honor society at school. You don't.

Your good friend isn't too choosy about whom he or she dates. Still, he or she is out most weekends while you stay home.

You practiced basketball two hours a day all summer. Your team's other point guard didn't practice at all. But when basketball season rolls around, the other point guard is named as the starter; you're on the bench again.

Some of your friends go shopping every weekend and actually have the money to buy new clothes every time. You used up your annual clothes budget before March.

You're expected to win your age bracket of the city tennis tournament. But you lose—in front of thousands of people—to someone you've beaten dozens of times before. He or she ends up winning the tournament. You come in third.

Because of your friend's parents' "connections," your friend will be getting a full scholarship to an exclusive private college. You're going to have to work like a dog just to go to a state school.

Mold Green	Apple Green	Pickle Green	Lizard Green	Hulk Green

II KINGS 2

The Heaven Express

Ahaziah, the king of Israel, injures himself in a fall and sends messengers to consult a pagan god to see if he will live. Elijah intercepts the messengers and instructs them to tell the king that he will die. A short time later, Elijah's prophecy is fulfilled. Accompanied by Elisha, Elijah makes a final visit to the prophets in Bethel and Jericho. Elijah is then dramatically whisked away to heaven in a whirlwind and a chariot of fire. Elisha symbolically picks up Elijah's cloak and carries on Elijah's work—including purifying a city's bad water and handling a large group of young men who refuse to show proper respect for God.

Have group members sit in a circle and take off their shoes. Blindfold group members or have them keep their eyes tightly closed. Mix up the shoes in the center of the circle. Conduct a contest to see who can find and put on a pair of shoes that aren't his or her own. Try this several times, since some group members may be a bit reluctant at first. Afterward, explain that while it may not have been easy to get in to someone else's shoes, it was probably even harder for Elisha to "walk in Elijah's shoes."

DATE I USED THIS SESSION _____ GROUP I USED IT WITH _____

NOTES FOR NEXT TIME _____

_____

_____

Q&A

1. If you were elected to an office, would you rather take over from someone who did a really good job or someone who did a pretty poor job? Why? Point out that Elisha faced the first challenge. Elijah had done an excellent job as prophet, and it would be a challenge to do as well.

2. Why do you think Elisha refused Elijah's requests to be alone (2:1-6)? (Perhaps Elisha knew that something was going to happen. It's not unusual for two close friends who are about to be separated to find it difficult to say good-bye.)

3. If you had been Elisha, knowing that Elijah was leaving and it was going to be up to you to replace him, how might you have felt at this point? Why?

4. Do you think Elisha truly hoped to be twice as powerful as Elijah (2:9, 10)? Explain. (Elisha wasn't requesting twice the greatness, but rather was wanting to be recognized as Elijah's successor. An oldest son would receive "a double portion" of a father's inheritance. Elisha wasn't trying to be greedy; he was committing himself to be Elijah's heir.)

5. Most people have a certain degree of fear about dying. But how do you think the way *we* get to heaven compares to Elijah's direct route (2:11, 12)? Which way would you rather go? Why?

6. Do you think Elisha got his wish to be a good successor to Elijah (2:13-18)? Explain. (Elisha began right away to perform the same miracles as Elijah. He also had a better understanding of what was going on than the rest of the prophets did.) To what extent do you think Elisha's success depended on his association with Elijah? (Elisha had been chosen to follow Elijah, but it was up to him to demonstrate the same degree of faith.)

7. The first thing Elisha did was purify some water in a bad spring (2:19-22). The action symbolized the purification that God wanted for His people. If you had the same opportunity, where do you think God might have you "sprinkle some salt" to purify a place that isn't particularly clean? Explain.

8. Elisha still didn't have the respect of all of the people—particularly the younger generation. In his culture, as in ours, thick hair was desirable. What can you tell about the youths who chided Elisha (2:23-25)? (These were young men rather than children. There were a lot of them, so it may have been a mass demonstration. Their taunting was as much at God as at Elisha.)

9. Do you think Elisha was justified in cursing the young men for making fun of him? What if we all did that? (Elisha was God's chosen representative. The scorn of the young men was therefore directed at God. Similarly, Jesus endured personal abuse, but got angry and took action when God's temple was shown disrespect.)

10. When God's messenger—Elisha—was treated with respect, God's blessing changed bad water to good. When he was scorned, the people experienced God's anger. What should we learn from this? (We need to treat other Christians with respect, beginning with local pastors and fellow youth group members.)

11. Would you have wanted Elisha's job? Why or why not?

Point out that regardless of the desirability of the job, Elisha's responsibilities were clear. With Elijah gone, it was now up to Elisha to bring God's message to the people—and to do whatever it took to show them that God was in control. The reproducible sheet, "Next in Command," challenges kids to put themselves in the same situation. Give kids a few minutes to work. When everyone is finished, let volunteers describe their full outline. If possible, ask *all* group members to share the problems they identified. (Their responses should help you target discussion topics for future sessions.) Explain that while the likelihood of your kids actually having to step in and take over for a pastor or youth leader may be slim at this point, they might want to think about trying it in the not-so-distant future. Try to get group members involved in ministry in new and different ways as frequently as possible.

Next in COMMAND

It finally happened. Your youth leaders, pastor, church board members, and Sunday school teachers were all at a meeting to try to plan ways to get young people more involved and excited about church. But you know how hard you guys are to please. So the harder they thought, the more their heads began to hurt, until . . . well, until their brains simultaneously short-circuited. The doctors say they'll be OK in three to four months, but until then, your leaders can't think about anything. All have been sent away to recuperate. The church and youth services are up to you. Everyone must plan at least one organized youth group meeting or church service.

Below is an outline that some leaders like to follow. (If you plan well enough, the teaching will take care of itself.) See how you do.

Purpose

What point do I want to get across to the group? What problem am I aware of that group members could use some help with?

Opening Activity

What would be a good game or opening activity to introduce the topic and get everyone excited?

Scripture

What would be some appropriate Bible stories or Scripture passages to study in regard to the previous point or problem?

Format

What's the best way to present the biblical material? (Lecture? Question and answer? Skit? Debate? Talk-show format?)

Application

What do I want people to do in response to what I'm trying to teach them?

Miscellaneous

What do I want to do about music? Refreshments? Are there any new, creative meeting places I'd like to try? What about guest speakers? What other ideas do I want to try?

II KINGS 4

Elisha's Believe It or Not

Elisha informs the kings of Israel, Judah, and Edom that the Lord will deliver Moab into their hands—which He does. As Elisha continues his ministry after Elijah's departure, his power is not only reminiscent of Elijah's previous work, but also offers a "preview" of the kinds of things Jesus will do. The miracles described in II Kings 4 include providing an ongoing supply of oil from a single jar, restoring a dead boy to life, providing an "antidote" to a poisonous pot of stew, and feeding one hundred people from a small supply of bread.

Hand out copies of "The Guinness Quiz of World Records." Give kids a few minutes to work; then go through the answers as a group. The correct answers (from the 1993 edition of *The Guinness Book of World Records*) are as follows: (1) c; (2) b; (3) c; (4) d; (5) a; (6) d; (7) d; (8) a; (9) b; (10) a. As an optional activity, you might have kids try to set some nonsensical world record. Afterward, point out that people are able to perform some pretty impressive feats with their own strength. But when God's people draw on God's power, they can do some truly *great* things—as will be seen during this session.

DATE I USED THIS SESSION _____ GROUP I USED IT WITH _____

NOTES FOR NEXT TIME _____

_____

_____

1. **If you were to receive a trophy today to honor the greatest achievement of your life so far, what accomplishment do you think would be noted?** Encourage group members to think beyond the things that normally get noticed and consider things such as "Most time devoted to youth events," "Most compassionate baby-sitter," "Best listener during Sunday sermons," and so forth. These and similar accomplishments *should* be noteworthy.

2. **If you had the miraculous power of God that Elisha demonstrated in II Kings 4, how would you use it? Why?**

3. **Do you think Elisha was ever tempted to use God's power to receive personal attention or recognition? Why or why not? If you were in Elisha's place, do you think you'd be tempted in that way? Why or why not?**

4. **What do you think Elisha was demonstrating to the widow with the "bottomless oil jar" miracle?** (The woman's husband had been a prophet. This was a way of showing her that God would still provide for her even though her husband had died.)

5. **How do you think the Shunammite woman felt when Elisha told her she would have a son (4:16)?** (Perhaps she thought it sounded too good to be true.) **How do you think she felt when her son was born (4:17)?** (She was probably overwhelmed with joy and thankfulness. Perhaps she was also a little ashamed that she'd doubted Elisha.) **How do you think she felt when her son died (4:18-21)?** (Perhaps she wondered why the Lord would raise her hopes, only to allow the child to die.)

6. **If you'd been the Shunammite woman, what would you have said to Elisha when you saw him?** Compare group members' responses with the woman's words in II Kings 4:28, 30.

7. **Why do you think Gehazi's efforts to revive the boy were unsuccessful?**

8. **Elisha knew that God was working through him. So**

why do you think he stopped to pray before doing anything (4:33)**?** (His prayer indicates that the power to raise the boy came from God alone, and not from Elisha.)

9. The men who had eaten the poisonous stew were prophets like Elisha. So why do you think they needed Elisha to miraculously remove the poison from the stew?

10. Compare Elisha's miracle in II Kings 4:42-44 with Jesus' miracle in Matthew 14:13-21. How are they similar? How are they different?

11. The people of Israel had received good things from God, yet had turned their backs on Him and sought out their own selfish pleasures, as well as other idols. Do you see any similarities between those people and the kids at your school? Do you see any major differences?

12. If someone like Elisha came to your school and started doing miraculous things, how do you think he would be received? Why? Do you think observing a few miracles would make people change the way they were living? Why or why not?

Point out that Elisha demonstrated that with God, a little oil goes a long way, a little bread goes a long way, a little flour goes a long way, and a little faith—well, it was enough to bring a dead boy back to life. We need to see that God frequently provides much more than we expect or ask for. Hand out paper and pencils. Down the left side of the paper, have kids list the things they *normally* include in their prayers: praises, thanksgiving, confessions, requests, and so forth. Then, down the right side of the paper, have kids list specific new things, particularly requests, that they'd like to include in their prayers. Encourage group members to pray faithfully each day this week for the things in both columns—and to add to the list each day. Explain that God doesn't always respond with a miracle, but if group members haven't been particularly close to Him lately, God's response may make such a difference in their lives that it *seems* like a miracle.

The Guinness Quiz of

WORLD RECORDS

1. In 1989, a Wisconsin woman heard of a birth in her family that made her a

(a) great great grandmother

(c) great great great great grandmother

(b) great great great grandmother

(d) great great great great great grandmother

2. In Memphis, Tennessee, in 1977, triplets were born within

(a) one minute

(c) five minutes

(b) two minutes

(d) ten minutes

3. The fastest flamenco dancer on record achieved

(a) 7 heel taps per second

(c) 16 heel taps per second

(b) 10 heel taps per second

(d) so much friction that his shoes caught fire

4. The world's largest dam (by volume) is in Argentina. It is 118 feet high and

(a) 8 miles long

(c) 81 miles long

(b) 18 miles long

(d) 108 miles long

5. In the suspension bridge category, California's Golden Gate is the world's

(a) tallest

(c) widest

(b) oldest

(d) longest

6. In 1989, a watch with 1,728 separate parts was sold in Switzerland for

(a) $515,500

(c) $2,456,608

(b) $1,826,000

(d) $3,315,000

7. In one second, the world-record yodeler produced

(a) 9 different tones

(c) 19 different tones

(b) 16 different tones

(d) 22 different tones

8. Something built at a community college in Alaska that was over 76 feet tall was

(a) a snowman

(c) a totem pole

(b) an igloo

(d) a house of cards

9. In eight hours, a person in India shook hands with

(a) 100,000 different people

(c) 15,006 different people

(b) 23,040 different people

(d) the heads of state of 132 different countries

10. A guy rode a unicycle for 38 seconds. The trick was that the wheel was

(a) 2.5 inches in diameter

(c) on a narrow track above a snake pit

(b) 10 feet in diameter

(d) made of metal rather than rubber

II KINGS 5

Naaman and the Seven Dips

Naaman, an officer in the army of the king of Aram, contracts leprosy. His wife has a servant—a young Israelite girl who is aware of the healing power of Elisha. Naaman makes a lot of effort to get in touch with Elisha, yet resents the instructions the prophet gives him and starts to reject them completely. Naaman's servants, however, convince him to obey, and his leprosy disappears. Naaman wants to reward Elisha, who refuses. But Elisha's servant, Gehazi, sees the opportunity for profit and secretly accepts gifts. As a result of his selfishness, Gehazi contracts leprosy that lasts the rest of his life.

The reproducible sheet, "Weird Doctor," contains a loosely constructed skit. Assign "diseases" (like those mentioned on the sheet) to various kids. Let one person play the doctor, who prescribes remedies as he or she sees fit. Give your "doctor" the sheet of "prescriptions," but encourage the person to be creative in devising new ideas. See how many kids are willing to actually do the ridiculous things they are asked to do. Use kids' responses to parallel what Naaman must have thought when instructed by Elisha to dip seven times in a dirty river.

DATE I USED THIS SESSION _____ GROUP I USED IT WITH _____

NOTES FOR NEXT TIME _____

_____

_____

Q&A

1. What's the strangest thing you've ever done on a dare or as an initiation? Why were you willing to do something so goofy—or maybe even dangerous?

2. Based on what you read in II Kings 5, do you think you would have liked Naaman? Why or why not? (He was a good soldier, but he was in an army that had fought against Israel. [There was a treaty at this time, but apparently border skirmishes were still taking place.] He seems like a proud man, perhaps impressed with his position. But in verse 15, he is humble enough to recognize God's power.)

3. Put yourself in the place of the servant girl. If you'd been captured by a foreign army and carried away from your home, how do you think you'd relate to the people who captured you? Why? If your owner's husband had leprosy, how would you feel? What do you think about the girl's willingness to help out her owners (5:2, 3)?

4. Now suppose that you're Naaman. You have leprosy. When you hear of a great healer, you make special arrangements to go see him (5:4-9). What would you expect when you got there?

5. How would you have felt if, after you finally found Elisha, he didn't even come out to see you? And what would you do if, on top of that, he sent word for you to go take a bath in a small, dirty river (5:10)? Compare kids' responses with Naaman's response in II Kings 5:11, 12.

6. Why do you think Naaman's servants were able to convince him to follow Elisha's "dippy" advice (5:13, 14)? (They convinced Naaman that he had nothing to lose by trying—except maybe his pride. Perhaps the servants better realized the importance of obedience than someone who was a leader of others.)

7. How do you think Naaman probably felt after his dips in the Jordan River (5:14)? (Of course he was relieved that his leprosy had been cured. But perhaps he was also emabarrassed at the way he'd stalked off after hearing Elisha's instructions.)

8. Why do you think Elisha refused Naaman's gifts? (Elisha wanted to make sure that all of the glory for Naaman's healing went to God.)

9. Do you think Gehazi's punishment fit his crime (5:20-27)? Why or why not? (Naaman's healing had been the result of God's grace. For Elisha [or Gehazi] to receive any kind of compensation would take away from God's free gift. As Elisha's assistant, Gehazi should have known better. Also, he compounded his greed with lies and deceit.)

10. Because of his pride, Naaman almost missed out on a miraculous healing. What kinds of things do people miss out on today because of pride and disobedience? (Refusing to obey God's simple instructions can cause people to miss out on a personal relationship with God and all of the peace, power, wisdom, and other benefits it provides.)

11. Does anything about your faith seem a bit ridiculous or confusing to you? If so, how do you respond to such issues? (We should strive to understand them. God doesn't want us to be confused. But at the same time, we need to remain obedient as we try to better understand God's instructions to us.)

Emphasize what a tragedy it was for Gehazi to lose his position with Elisha because of a greedy attitude. Then explain that the temptation remains for all Christians today. Ask: **What problems might someone expect if he or she develops a "What's in it for me?" attitude toward Christianity?** Don't rush this. Kids may see that greed and selfishness diminish God's grace, cause every little problem to seem unfair, give the wrong idea to others who see us, and so forth. Then ask: **What feelings can you expect if you begin a "What's in it for other people?" attitude toward your faith?** Kids may discover that many of the things they want for themselves (fulfillment, joy, closer friendships, and so forth) can only take place when they begin to put others before themselves. Challenge kids to begin this week to make any needed shifts in emphasis in their lives.

WEIRD DOCTOR

This is a skit in which you, the weird doctor, get to prescribe strange remedies for people who come to you with their ailments. Your group leader will assign various "diseases"—such as hiccups, migraine headaches, leprosy, mononucleosis, boils in unusual places, hangnails, dry skin, broken arms, and so forth—to fellow group members. When they come to you, suggest one of the following remedies or come up with better ones. The "patients" won't have to do what you tell them, so try not to go too far. But see what you can get away with.

HERE ARE SOME POSSIBLE PRESCRIPTIONS:

• Draw your face on a sheet of paper, cut out eye holes and a mouth hole, and then tape it over your face for three minutes.

• Let three people punch you in the arm four times each.

• Keep your eyes closed and stand on one foot for three minutes.

• Do one hundred jumping jacks.

• Hold a pencil between your teeth until you're told to take it out.

• Take off your shoes and run around the room backward five times.

• Give away all of your loose change to other people.

• Let someone "wheelbarrow race" you around the room four times.

• Stand on a chair and sing the national anthem at the top of your lungs.

• For the next three minutes, using body language and sound effects, imitate a chicken trying to lay an egg.

• Put ice on the afflicted area and keep it there until the ice melts.

• Say the alphabet backward six times.

• Go around the room singing, "I'm a Little Teapot"—while performing the appropriate motions—until you're told to stop.

• Sniff the right shoe of everyone in the room. (Shoes must first be taken off.)

Safe and Surrounded

Elisha continues to demonstrate the power of God as well as the depth of his own spiritual understanding. First, he causes a lost iron axhead to float to the top of a river. Then, when a servant panics after he and Elisha appear to be vastly outnumbered, Elisha reveals the extent of God's protective forces. He then peacefully captures an entire army that had been sent specifically to capture *him*.

Hand out copies of the reproducible sheet, "Do You See What I See?" Let group members examine the optical illusions to see how their eyes may occasionally deceive them. (The correct answers are as follows: [1] B; [2] A; [3] Both are the same length; [4] A.) Later, refer to these illusions as you discuss *spiritual* perspective. If our spiritual "vision" is not working, or is out of focus, we may miss out on a lot. But if we begin to see more of the things God provides and the way He works in our lives, the "big picture" becomes a lot clearer and makes more sense.

DATE I USED THIS SESSION _____ GROUP I USED IT WITH _____

NOTES FOR NEXT TIME _____

_____

_____

1. Have you ever borrowed something of value from someone, only to lose or damage it? If so, how did you feel? How did the person who loaned it to you feel when you explained what had happened?

2. Elisha had already saved the prophets from a pot of poisoned stew (4:38-41). Now he solved the problem of the lost axhead (6:4-7). If you'd been one of the other prophets, how do you think you would have felt about having Elisha around? Why?

3. What made Elisha such an excellent military strategist (6:8-10)? (He always knew where Israel's enemies were, and could advise the king to avoid those places.) **If you were the leader of a military force opposing Israel, what would be your strategy?** Compare group members' responses with the king of Aram's strategy in II Kings 6:11-14.

4. Put yourself in Elisha's servant's place. What do you think it might have been like to awaken to find yourself surrounded by an entire army—sent exclusively to get the person you're hanging around with (6:15)? What do you think you might have done in such a situation?

5. In what situations today do you think Elisha's words in II Kings 6:16 might provide comfort?

6. After *telling* his servant that all was well, Elisha decided to let him see for himself (6:17). Do you think this new awareness made a difference in the servant's attitude? Why or why not?

7. How does it make *you* feel to know that at this very moment you might be surrounded by invisible forces of God that are far more numerous and powerful than anything else you will ever encounter?

8. How do you think the Arameans felt when Elisha told them that they were in the wrong place? How do you think they felt when their eyes were opened and they found themselves in Samaria?

9. Suppose you're at school and a group of your opponents are giving you a hard time. If they were suddenly blinded and you could see clearly, what would you do? (Run; stick around to torment them; make fun of them and then leave; etc.) Compare group members' responses to Elisha's actions in II Kings 6:19-23.

10. Can you think of a situation that you're currently facing for which conflict seems to be the only way out—if there seems to be a way out at all? If so, what's the situation? With further thought, do you think there's *any* opportunity for a peaceful and lasting resolution of the problem? If so, what would need to happen?

Suggest that we are too seldom like Elisha and too often like his servant. We see problems and not solutions. We think in terms of power and revenge rather than forgiveness and compassion. Certainly your group members will face problems that have no easy answers, but many of their dilemmas would be better resolved if the people involved would simply remember that the power and peace of God are available to them. Have group members think of some sign or token they can literally carry with them during the next week to remind them of God's presence in their lives. It could be as simple as a string tied around a finger, a bookmark with the reminder to "Open your eyes," a friendship bracelet to remind them of God's friendship, or any number of things. During the week as they face problems and struggles, challenge them to remember to pray for God to open their spiritual eyes and give them a better perspective on each situation—a perspective that includes hope and confidence.

Do You See What I See?

Below are a few optical illusions. After you've figured out each of them, try to think of some spiritual lessons we might be able to learn from optical illusions.

1. In which figure are all of the long diagonal lines parallel?

A

B

C

2. In which figure are the two horizontal lines parallel?

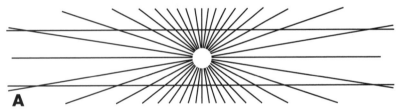
A

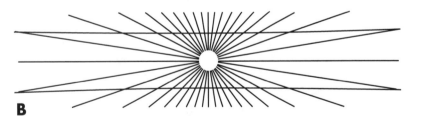
B

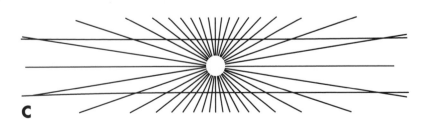
C

3. Which horizontal line is longer?

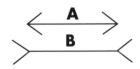

4. In which figure are the two diagonals equal in length?

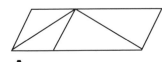
A

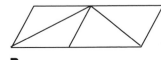
B

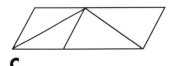
C

II KINGS 18–20

Empty Threats

In the midst of a great famine in Israel, the Lord causes the Arameans to desert their camp, thus allowing the people of Israel to raid the food and belongings of the Arameans. During Joash's reign in Judah, the temple is rebuilt. During Hoshea's reign in Israel, Israel is conquered by the Assyrians. The people of Israel are exiled to Assyria. The Assyrians then lay siege to Judah. The Assyrians publicly threaten the people in an attempt to undermine Judah's confidence in God and King Hezekiah. But the prophet Isaiah assures King Hezekiah that Assyrian King Sennacherib's efforts will fail. True to the prophecy, an angel of God kills 185,000 Assyrians in a single night and the threat is removed. Hezekiah later falls ill and is told that he will not recover. But he prays, and God gives him another fifteen years to live.

The reproducible sheet, "Sweatin' to the Threats," contains a number of scenarios for kids to roleplay. Read each scenario, designate some people to act out the roles, and see how kids would handle that threatening situation. Feel free to add other scenarios if you know of specific threatening circumstances your young people are facing. Try to put them in some realistic settings so that group members will better relate to the people of Judah, who received the threats of Sennacherib.

DATE I USED THIS SESSION _____ GROUP I USED IT WITH _____

NOTES FOR NEXT TIME _____

_____

_____

1. Suppose you go to a party where there's all kinds of out-of-control behavior going on. People are drinking, doing drugs, having sex in the upstairs bedrooms, gossiping, and doing pretty much everything else you can think of. You might be shocked to witness such things, but what, if anything, would you *do*? Why?

2. The kings of Israel and Judah had become a series of "party people," caring more about themselves and their false gods than for the true God. Hezekiah was the first king in a long time to change things (18:1-8.). **Do you think his changes made him more popular with the people or less popular? Explain.** (If the people of Judah didn't approve of his changes at first, they certainly did later when God miraculously delivered them from the Assyrians.)

3. The Assyrians conquered Israel (18:9-12) and then came after Judah. Hezekiah paid a tribute to try to avoid battle (18:13-16), but soon Sennacherib, the King of Assyria, demanded full surrender. What do you think of the methods the King of Assyria used to try to shake up the people of Judah (18:17-25)? Explain.

4. If you had been one of the people of Judah, how might you have responded to the message of the Assyrians (18:19-25)? Why? Which of the statements in the message would have affected you the most? Why?

5. Do you think Isaiah's assurance that the Lord would defeat the Assyrians (19:6, 7) had any effect on the people of Judah? If so, what effect did it have? If not, why not?

6. Which parts of Isaiah's prophecy (19:21-34) do you think meant the most to King Hezekiah? Why?

7. Sometime after this event, King Hezekiah faced another crisis—this time of a more personal nature (20:1). If you received the news that Hezekiah received from Isaiah, what would you do?

8. Isaiah's prophecies had always been accurate. So when Hezekiah received word that he would not recover from his illness, why do you think he ignored Isaiah's instructions to "put [his] house in order" (20:1)? Why do you think he appealed to God instead (20:2, 3)? (Hezekiah had been faithful to God and felt he could now be completely honest with Him.)

9. Do you think God changed His mind regarding Hezekiah's death (20:4-11)? How would you explain God's decision to add fifteen years to Hezekiah's life when originally He had said that Hezekiah would not recover? (The importance of prayer even in situations that seem hopeless should not be overlooked here.)

10. If you could request a sign from God to prove that He will do what He promises, what sign would you choose? Why?

11. Hezekiah certainly wasn't perfect (20:12-21). But do you think the fact that he was a good and faithful king had any effect on God's willingness to let him live another fifteen years? Do you think faithfulness to God extends life today? Explain. (Perhaps not in as direct a manner, but people who live according to God's guidelines can certainly expect a longer life [on average] than those who don't. Drinking, drug use, promiscuous sex, and other such habits can reduce life expectancy.)

(Needed: Balloons and markers)

Suggest that Hezekiah shows us the right way to deal with threats. He faced almost certain defeat by the Assyrians and then almost certain death. Yet in both cases, he turned to God instead of panicking. Provide balloons of assorted sizes. Ask kids to identify some of their own threatening circumstances. Let everyone inflate balloons to appropriate sizes and label them with markers to indicate any people, things, or situations that currently seem threatening. Then pray together, asking God for faith to face all of these threats and affirming that He is more than capable of dealing with them. After the prayer, close the session by popping or stomping all of the "threats."

Sweatin' to the Threats

Below are some roleplays that involve threatening situations. In each case, you can add anyone you wish to the roleplay. For example, if you would go to a friend in one situation, call on someone to play that role for you. If you need parents, pastors, hit-men, or anyone else, feel free to designate people before the roleplay begins.

1. Last Friday night, you spent the night at a friend's house. Your friend had received a camera as a birthday present the day before. The two of you spent some time checking out the camera, during which time your friend took a picture of you doing something extremely embarrassing. Your friend is threatening to make copies of the picture and display them around school for everyone to see on your birthday, which is two days from now. What would you do?

2. You and a couple of friends have decided to try to have a small Bible study during lunch hour at school. The weather is good, so you find a remote area on the lawn beneath a tree. You're a little bit uncomfortable with being so "public," but you feel it's something you should do. The first two meetings go well. But now, as you're concluding the third one, some of the school tough guys/girls have figured out what's going on. They come out and start harassing you. They make remarks like "There's not much we like better than beating up on Christians" and "You won't be meeting out here again, will you?" How would you respond?

4. One day after school, you make your way to the rest room before catching the bus home. As you enter the rest room, you see money and several bags of some white powder changing hands. You realize you've just witnessed a drug deal taking place. You notice that several of the kids involved are well-known gang members at your school. As they stare menacingly at you, you mutter some incoherent gibberish and quickly turn on your heels to leave the rest room. However, they grab you before you can get away. They tell you that if you breathe a word to anyone about what you've just seen, you'll be "dead meat." What would you do?

3. Because you've been falling behind in your advanced math class, you've been staying after school a few days a week for some extra tutoring with your teacher. During one of these tutorial sessions, your teacher makes an obvious sexual advance toward you. Feeling extremely uncomfortable, you grab your books and quickly head for the door. As you're leaving, your teacher says that if you tell anyone about what happened, your grade will suffer. What would you do?

5. Describe a threatening situation of your own to roleplay.

_____
_____
_____
_____
_____
_____
_____
_____
_____
_____

II KINGS 22–23

The Word Is Out

After King Hezekiah dies, Manasseh succeeds him and leads Judah back into idol worship. Later, Josiah, a good king, sees that the temple has been neglected for a long time and arranges to have it repaired. During the cleanup, the high priest finds the Book of the Law, which has been forgotten. After reading God's standards of living, Josiah is humbled and distraught. Because of Josiah's repentant attitude, God postpones His judgment. Josiah begins to restore the spiritual integrity of Judah—destroying idols, killing evil priests, and even reestablishing the Passover. Yet after Josiah dies, Judah quickly returns to a state of spiritual wickedness.

(Needed: Miscellaneous "treasures")

Before kids arrive, hide an assortment of "treasures"—coins, fast food certificates, dollar bills, etc. To begin the session, announce: **This room is filled with treasure. See how much of it you can find.** As kids find things, say: **Keep looking. There's more treasure here.** Afterward, have kids vote on the most valuable treasure they found. Then announce that their Bibles *ought* to be considered treasure. In this session, they'll see what happens when Scripture is ignored or taken for granted.

DATE I USED THIS SESSION _____ GROUP I USED IT WITH _____

NOTES FOR NEXT TIME _____

_____

_____

1. How many of you think you could run this country if you were given an opportunity? What would you need to do before you felt confident about running the country? What would you expect your biggest problems to be? Point out that Josiah became king when he was eight years old (22:1, 2) and did an excellent job.

2. How do you think Josiah knew to do "what was right in the eyes of the Lord" (22:2) when his father, Amon, "did evil in the eyes of the Lord" (21:20)?

3. Why do you think the temple was allowed to become run down and the Book of the Law was allowed to remain missing for so many years (22:3-8)?

4. Do you find Josiah's reaction to hearing God's law (22:11-13) **natural or a bit unusual? Why?** (Josiah had been trying to be obedient to God, yet the expectations spelled out in the law were very specific—as were the consequences of disobeying. His grief was genuine, though it might seem unusual to some people.)

5. Sometimes we may wonder if our attitudes really make a difference when we keep them to ourselves. **Based on II Kings 22:14-20, do you think a good attitude is necessary as long as our actions are OK? Explain.** (God was aware that Josiah's "heart was responsive" and rewarded him. Proper attitudes are *very* important.)

6. If you had been promised that you personally would avoid the destruction that was coming to your country, how do you think such knowledge would affect your lifestyle? (Some people might take it easy and relax. But Josiah worked hard to repair the spiritual damage that had been done in the past [22:20–23:27].)

7. Josiah's first priority was to make sure *everyone* heard God's Word, so he read it to them (23:1-3). Can you think of any parts of the Bible that are "lost" to you because you know so little about them? If so, how can you "find" those important sections of Scripture?

8. Next, Josiah eliminated everything that Scripture said was wrong (23:4-20, 24). Can you think of any behavior you've recently eliminated because the Bible said it was sinful? Does anything in your life still need to be eliminated? If so, what is it?

9. Josiah also reestablished required practices that had been abandoned, such as Passover (23:21-23). Can you think of anything you used to enjoy about Christianity that you've quit doing? If so, how might you get started again?

10. Josiah was a good king at a crucial time in Judah's history. But the kings who followed him were evil and returned to the sinful things that Josiah had worked so hard to eliminate (23:26-37). Are there any negative influencers in your life who seem to "drag you down" every time you try to be a more godly person? If so, what are some ways to deal with such people?

Suggest that Josiah's actions provide a good model for all of us. Hand out copies of the reproducible sheet, "Read It and Weep." Spend some time helping group members work through the cycle described on the sheet. (You might start with II Kings 22 and 23, the material covered in this session. The last few questions of the session should have worked through the cycle already.) Then spend some time helping group members find a good "starting point" from their "lost" portions of the Bible. If, for instance, they never read prophecy, you might suggest the Book of Jonah, some of Isaiah's chapters predicting the coming of Jesus, or other highlights. If you help them start with an interesting and self-explanatory portion of Scripture, they are much more likely to keep trying to study on their own.

READ It AND weep

When King Josiah found the lost law of God and read it for the first time in years, he felt great dismay and remorse because the Scripture pointed out all of the things that were wrong with his kingdom. Of course, he had a pretty good excuse, since the scroll had been lost. Most people today have access to a Bible, yet God's Word remains "lost" when we don't bother to read it. The Bible is filled with good stuff, but a lot of it remains lost to us because we're too quick to label it "boring" or "hard to understand." Yet if we follow Josiah's example, we might make our world a much better place to live. Try the following cycle of progress to see what happens.

Step 1: READ
Identify a section of the Bible that remains "lost" to you because you haven't bothered to try reading it in a long, long time (if ever). Then find a good story in that section to see what you discover. (Ask for help if you need to!) *Some ideas might include:*

Step 4: REESTABLISH
Look for things you ought to be doing—perhaps things you used to do that you need to start doing again. *Some ideas might include:*

Step 2: REMOVE
Look for things you may be doing now that don't agree with what God says in His Word. If you have "idols" of your own, get rid of them! *Some ideas might include:*

Step 3: REPAIR
Sometimes the Bible will point out things we could be doing better, even if we're already doing a pretty good job of obeying. We need to continually work to do everything God wants us to do. *Some ideas might include:*

II KINGS 25

Here Comes the Judgment

All of the prophecies of Judah's destruction finally come to pass as Nebuchadnezzar and the Babylonians besiege Jerusalem. The palace and God's temple are ransacked and burned. The poorest people are left to tend the land while the others are taken back to Babylon as captives. The Judahite leader left in charge and his associates are assassinated by jealous fellow countrymen. The people of Judah then flee to Egypt for safety.

Hand out copies of the reproducible sheet, "Judge . . . Not!" to kids willing to perform the skit. Afterward, ask: **How would you feel to witness such decisions from a courtroom judge?** (Most would be shocked by such atrocious rulings from a judge who knows the law and is sworn to uphold it.) **Why do you think so many people get angry at God when He acts as a judge whose role is to punish sinful people?** (Even though God is compassionate and forgiving, He holds people accountable for their actions. If He didn't, God would deserve no more respect than the judge in the skit.) **Do you think people use similar excuses with God? Explain.**

DATE I USED THIS SESSION _____ GROUP I USED IT WITH _____

NOTES FOR NEXT TIME_____

_____

_____

1. Have you ever been in a situation in which you were absolutely sure that something bad was going to happen, but you didn't know exactly when? If so, what were the circumstances? How did you feel while you were waiting? What finally happened?

2. God had sent prophets to tell His people of the consequences of their evil ways. One eventual consequence would involve being captured by foreign nations and exiled away from their own country. Israel was defeated by the Assyrians, and now the Babylonians were attacking Judah. If the people knew of God's judgment, why do you think they bothered to put up a fight (II Kings 25:1-3)? (Some of the leaders *did* advise them to go with the Babylonians and try to make the best of their exile [25:24]. But the people had ignored God all along, and they still weren't listening.)

3. Suppose your city is under siege. Due to a famine, your forces are weak and depleted. You've heard commotion outside the city limits for months, and finally the invading armies storm in. What do you think would happen at that point? Compare group members' responses with Nebuchadnezzar's brutal actions in II Kings 25:4-12.

4. Saddest of all, the temple was stormed, the valuable and sacred furnishings were stolen, and the building was burned (25:9, 13-17). If our meeting area were destroyed in a fire—building, song books, instruments, and everything—how do you think we would cope? Explain. What would we do?

5. The leaders of Judah were first taken captive and then executed (25:18-21). Do you think that was necessary? Why or why not? (Perhaps they were killed in order to prevent a rebellion.) How do you think our church would function without its leaders? Why?

6. Nebuchadnezzar still wanted control over the people left behind in Judah, so he appointed Gedaliah—a leader of Judah who had previously recommended cooperation with the Babylonians—to oversee them (25:22-24). Would you like to have had Gedaliah's job? Why or why not? (Even though Gedaliah saw the situation from God's perspective, his advice might have seemed treasonous to some people.)

7. **Sure enough, another person from Judah, Ishmael—who probably had hopes for leadership—assassinated Gedaliah and his followers (25:25, 26). Even with all of the turmoil the nation had just gone through, Ishmael was scheming to get ahead. Do you know people who rarely seem to be concerned with anything other than themselves? If so, what techniques do they use to get ahead?**

8. **At this point, do you think things could get any worse for God's people? Would you expect things to get any better for a while?** If no one mentions it, point out that at least the Babylonians began to show respect for one of Judah's kings who had been captured (25:27-30). It was a glimmer of hope that David's royal line would not be permanently extinguished.

9. **Continual sin caused the people of Israel and Judah to face God's judgment. What can we learn from the Israelites' example?**

10. **What are some specific things you can do to prevent your sins from accumulating like those of Israel and Judah?** Compile a master list, and make copies for everyone, if appropriate.

While many of the events in this chapter were quite brutal, don't let kids leave with the impression that God is eager to strike people down for any little mistake. Ask: **Why do you think God disciplines people who sin?** (It's for their good, not His pleasure.) **What methods does God use to discipline people?** Compile a list of kids' responses. Among other things, they might mention "loss of peace," "confusion as to direction in life," and so forth. Close the session by having someone read Hebrews 12:4-13. This passage should help group members see the "discipline" of God in a positive light.

JUDGE: Bailiff, announce the next case.

BAILIFF: State versus Brandon. It's a kidnapping case, your honor.

PROSECUTOR: Pet kidnapping, actually, your honor. Mike Brandon was caught stealing all of the pets in his neighborhood. He was planning to sell them to buy drugs. We have all of the evidence right here.

JUDGE: Sounds guilty to me. What do you have to say, Mr. Defense Attorney?

DEFENDER: Your honor, Mike is from a good home. The Brandons are excellent citizens who have a good reputation. Can't you give him a break?

JUDGE: OK. Sure. Not guilty!

PROSECUTOR: But, your honor, that's not fair!

JUDGE: Don't argue with me or I'll fine you for contempt. Bailiff, next case!

BAILIFF: State versus Larson twins. The charge is arson.

PROSECUTOR: Your honor, Carson and Marsha Larson were caught while setting fire to a nursing home. The gasoline cans and matches were in their possession. But not only did they set fire to the building, they also hung around to trip the people trying to get out.

DEFENDER: All of this is true, your honor, but no one was hurt. The building suffered only minor damage. And my clients both say they're very sorry.

CARSON LARSON: Besides, Judge, it was rather comical to see all of those old people scrambling out with their walkers, canes, crutches, and such.

MARSHA LARSON: Yeah, since no one was hurt, can we go? I've got a tennis lesson.

JUDGE: I guess insurance will cover the damages. OK, case dismissed! Bailiff?

BAILIFF: The next case is Miller versus Miller. Attempted murder.

PROSECUTOR: Your honor, surely this case will require your firm hand of justice. The Miller children, Sonny and Cher, repeatedly disobeyed their parents' instructions, curfews, and warnings. When the parents finally cracked down and tried to ground them, both kids picked up fireplace pokers and beat the parents unconscious. If a neighbor hadn't overheard and called the police, these kids would have killed both parents.

JUDGE: My, this does sound serious. What have you to say, Mr. D.A.?

DEFENDER: Your honor, my clients are young and impetuous. Don't you remember how you were at that age? We all go through periods of anger and confusion. How can we punish only two people for what we all feel?

SONNY MILLER: Yeah, Judge. We're young. We've got a lot more time to commit senseless violent acts before we're old enough to deserve *hard* time.

CHER MILLER: Yeah, you old bag of wind. Let us go free or I'll go on *Soft Copy* to tell everyone how unfair the system is and how it's your fault.

JUDGE: I see what you mean, Mr. Defense Attorney. These young rapscallions have a madcap attitude toward authority. I ought to put them away for several years or at least require them to seek serious psychological help. But, hey, the jails are full anyway. Why overcrowd them further? Not guilty! Bailiff, what's next?

BAILIFF: We have a case in which nine people videotaped the suspect hitting, kicking, shooting, stabbing, poisoning, and then spitting on the victim.

PROSECUTOR: Never mind, your honor. I'm withdrawing the case. I give up.

DEFENDER: It's for the best anyway, Judge. He says the devil made him do it.

EZRA

Back to Jerusalem

[NOTE: Because I and II Chronicles are made up primarily of material found in other books of the Old Testament, we've omitted them from our book-by-book format.]

King Cyrus, the ruler of Persia (who had conquered the Babylonians who had exiled the people of Judah), allows the exiled Israelites to return to Jerusalem. The people in the first expedition rebuild the altar and begin to rebuild the temple. Their work on the temple is delayed by a new king, Artaxerxes. Construction continues several years later under King Darius; the temple is completed and dedicated. When Ezra, a godly teacher, arrives in Jerusalem with a second expedition, he discovers that the Israelites have intermarried with people from other nations who practice idolatry and commit other evil deeds. Ezra is so distraught by this discovery that his weeping causes the Israelites to repent of their sin.

Distribute copies of the reproducible sheet, "Odd Couples." Give kids a few minutes to complete the sheet. When everyone is finished, ask volunteers to share what they came up with. Then point out that when the Israelites got back to Israel, they started forming "odd couples" by marrying people of foreign nations—something God had expressly forbidden.

DATE I USED THIS SESSION _____ GROUP I USED IT WITH _____

NOTES FOR NEXT TIME _____

_____

_____

1. What's the biggest cleanup project you've ever tackled? How did the project go?

2. How do you think the Israelites responded when King Cyrus made his proclamation (1:1-4)? Why do you suppose King Cyrus allowed the Israelites to return to Jerusalem?

3. If you'd been one of the Israelites in the first expedition back to Jerusalem (Ezra 2), what might have been going through your mind during the journey? Explain.

4. Why do you suppose the altar was rebuilt first (3:1-6)? Why do you think the laying of the foundation of the temple was such an emotional event for the Israelites—especially for some of the older priests, Levites, and family heads (3:11-13)?

5. Why do you think the "enemies" of Judah and Benjamin wanted to help with the rebuilding of the temple (4:1, 2)? Why do you think the Israelites denied their request (4:3)? (Perhaps the enemies had ulterior motives—like plans for idol worship—in making their offer.)

6. Why was the accusation that the enemies of Judah and Benjamin lodged with King Artaxerxes so potentially damaging (4:6-16)? (The accusation suggested that the Israelites would become traitorous to Persia when they finished rebuilding their city.) What kinds of damaging accusations do people make today? What is the best way to respond to such accusations?

7. What do you think the day of dedication for the temple was like (6:16-18)? Explain.

8. When Ezra found out that some of the Jewish men had married foreign women, he repented before God (9:1-15). Why do you think Ezra repented when he hadn't done anything wrong?

9. What do you think of Ezra's response to the sins of the Israelites (10:1, 6)? Do you think he was overreacting a

little? Why or why not? (It seems as if the Israelites had become "numb" to their sin. Ezra's startling actions shook them up. His actions drove home the point that what the Israelites had done was terrible in God's sight.) **If a new pastor came to your church and reacted to the sins of the congregation in the same way that Ezra responded to the Israelites' sins, how do you think the people of the church would respond? How would you respond? Why?**

10. Ezra 10:8 describes the penalties that Ezra set for anyone who failed to assemble in Jerusalem within three days. If God were to send someone like Ezra to today's society, what methods might the person use to insure that everyone would meet together to hear what was said?

11. The list of the people who had married foreign women included religious leaders who should have known better. Among them were priests, Levites, gatekeepers, and temple singers (10:18-44). **How do you think high-ranking, well-trained leaders like these got involved in doing what they knew was wrong?**

12. Why do people today get involved in doing things they know are wrong?

Point out that God had warned the Israelites many times about intermarrying with people of foreign nations—but the Israelites continued to do so. Contrast the extreme reaction of Ezra to the people's sins with the reaction of the people themselves, who seemed almost oblivious to the problem. Then ask kids to think of a particular sin in their lives that they keep going back to—perhaps lying, gossiping, or something more serious (and personal). Ask: **What might happen if you responded to this sin in the way that Ezra responded to the Israelites' sins? What would it take for you to get to the point where you could respond in an Ezra-like way?** Close the session in prayer, asking God to convict group members of recurring sins in their lives and thanking Him for the fact that He is willing not only to forgive our sins, but also to help us overcome our tendency to sin.

Odd Couples

Some things just don't belong together. In the categories below, come up with the two most unusual, disgusting, or unexpected items that you can imagine being paired together. Be as creative as possible in your answers.

1. The two worst toppings to put together on a pizza would be _____ and _____.

2. The weirdest pairing of actors or actresses in a movie would be _____ and _____.

3. The most disgusting drink imaginable would be a mixture of _____ and _____.

4. The most unusual first-and-middle-name combination to give to a baby would be _____ and _____.

5. The most unlikely couple to get married would be _____ and _____.

6. The weirdest pair of singers to record a duet would be _____ and _____.

7. The two most disgusting foods to eat together would be _____ and _____.

8. Two physical movements that can't be done at the same time are _____ and _____.

9. Two people who should never be invited to the same party are _____ and _____.

10. Two other things that should never be combined are _____ and _____.

NEHEMIAH 1–3

The Wall

Shortly after Ezra's arrival in Jerusalem, Nehemiah, an Israelite living in Babylon and a member of the court of King Artaxerxes, receives news that the walls of Jerusalem had been completely destroyed, leaving the city vulnerable to attack. Nehemiah is so upset by this news that, after a time of prayer and fasting, he asks King Artaxerxes to allow him to go to Jerusalem to supervise the rebuilding of the walls. With the king's permission, Nehemiah heads for Jerusalem.

(Needed: Prizes)

Hold a contest to see which of your kids is best at breaking bad news. Have kids imagine that some kind of accident or disaster has occurred and it's their job to break the news to someone who's affected by it. For instance, you might give the following scenario: **While your next-door neighbors are on vacation, their house burns down. That night, they call your house to find out how things are going. No one else is home, so you have to break the bad news to them. How would you do it?** Award prizes for the most creative method of breaking the news, the most sensitive method, and the most humorous method. Use this activity to lead in to a discussion of the bad news that Nehemiah received in Nehemiah 1:3.

DATE I USED THIS SESSION _____ GROUP I USED IT WITH _____

NOTES FOR NEXT TIME _____

_____

_____

1. What's the longest amount of time you've ever been away from home? While you were away, did you receive any letters or phone calls giving you news about home? If so, how did they make you feel? Why?

2. Why do you think Nehemiah was so upset by the news he received from Jerusalem (1:3, 4)? (The fact that the walls were destroyed meant that Jerusalem was completely vulnerable to attack from its enemies.)

3. What can you tell about Nehemiah from his prayer to God in Nehemiah 1:5-11? Explain. (He was humble before God. He was aware of the Israelites' history of disobedience to God. He was also aware of God's covenants with Israel.)

4. Hand out copies of the reproducible sheet, "Reading between the Lines." Give group members a few minutes to read through it. **Would you have taken a job as cupbearer to the king during Nehemiah's day? Why or why not?**

5. Praying and planning seemed to go hand in hand for Nehemiah. When the king asked what Nehemiah wanted, Nehemiah first prayed, then presented a clear plan of action to the king (2:4-9). What might have happened if Nehemiah had left out either part of that equation? Explain.

6. Why do you think King Artaxerxes allowed his cupbearer to go running off to build a wall around some foreign city?

7. How do you think Nehemiah reacted when he first saw Jerusalem? Explain.

8. Nehemiah's plan for rebuilding the walls faced opposition, particularly from Sanballat and Tobiah, a couple of area tribal leaders. Nehemiah says these two "mocked and ridiculed" the workers (2:19). How do you deal with people like this in your life?

9. Based on the list of workers given in Nehemiah 3, how would you anticipate the reconstruction of the wall turning out? (Many of the people who worked on the wall—including priests [3:1], perfume makers [3:8], and goldsmiths [3:31] probably had little, if any, construction background.) **What can we learn from this?** (God can use anyone—regardless of background or training—to accomplish His work.)

10. **What do you think of Nehemiah's management style? Explain.** (By allowing many different people—and not just skilled professionals—to help rebuild the wall, Nehemiah insured that the Israelite people would have a vested interest in the completion of the project. And with so many people working on the wall, it was probably completed much sooner than if skilled laborers had been assigned to do it.)

11. **What traits of good leadership do we see in Nehemiah's example in Nehemiah 1–3?** (Nehemiah was a person of prayer; he developed a plan; he had vision [from God]; he kept some things to himself [2:12]; etc.)

Remind group members that Nehemiah's success was due to prayer and planning. Hand out paper and pencils. Ask group members to write down one major project that they are currently facing or will be facing in the future. After a few minutes, collect the sheets. One at a time, read the responses aloud. Then, as a group, come up with a "plan of attack" for tackling each project. Afterward, close the session in prayer, asking God to give your group members the wisdom and strength to tackle their projects.

READING *between the Lines*

Sometimes we read things that seem obvious at first glance. But when we really understand what's happening, we can see some amazing stuff. Below are some excerpts from Nehemiah 1 and 2, as well as some "between the lines" information that may help you see what a big deal it was for Nehemiah to approach King Artaxerxes to ask for permission to go to Jerusalem.

"I was cupbearer to the king" (1:11).

The cupbearer was responsible to sample the king's food before the king ate it to insure that the food wasn't poisoned. Because the king's life was literally in the cupbearer's hands, it was a position held by only the most trusted advisors.

"In the month of Nisan . . ." (2:1)

No, this was not some month-long car sales promotion. Nisan was one of the months on the Persian calendar. Nehemiah had first heard about the problem in Jerusalem during the month of Kislev (1:1), which was four months earlier. This would seem to indicate that Nehemiah had been praying, planning, and waiting for the right time to approach the king with his idea.

"I had not been sad in [the king's] presence before; so the king asked me, 'Why does your face look so sad when you are not ill? This can be nothing but sadness of heart.' I was very much afraid" (2:1, 2).

An interesting law among the Persians stated that no one was to be sad in the king's presence. The penalty for being sad without a good reason before the king was death. So Nehemiah had good reason to fear when the king noticed his sad face.

NEHEMIAH 4–6

Wall-to-Wall Opposition

After securing permission from King Artaxerxes to repair Jerusalem's walls, Nehemiah returns to Jerusalem to oversee the project. During the construction, Nehemiah faces opposition from neighboring tribes outside the city who view the rebuilding of the wall as a sign of the Israelites' asserting their independence. Nehemiah also discovers problems between the Israelites that hamper their ability to work together.

(Needed: Prepared slips of paper, game items)

Before the session, prepare several slips of paper. On one slip, write some kind of instruction (e.g., "Shoot five paper wads into the trash can"). On another slip of paper, write an opposite instruction (e.g., "Do not allow anyone to shoot paper wads into the trash can"). Make sure that each instruction you come up with has an opposite instruction. As kids arrive, hand each of them a slip. Give them five minutes to complete their task. Afterward, point out that Nehemiah faced opposition when he tried to complete his assigned task of rebuilding the walls of Jerusalem.

DATE I USED THIS SESSION _____ GROUP I USED IT WITH _____

NOTES FOR NEXT TIME _____

_____

_____

1. Have you ever been ridiculed or harrassed for doing something you thought was right? If so, what were the circumstances? How did the ridicule and harrassment affect you? How did the situation turn out?

2. Sanballat and Tobiah, the leaders of neighboring tribes, harrassed Nehemiah and the Israelites during their rebuilding of the Jerusalem walls (4:1-11). **Why do you think these guys were so concerned about the Israelites' construction project?** (The rebuilding of the walls may have been seen as a sign of the Israelites' trying to assert their independence. The walls also would have prevented Sanballat and Tobiah from attacking and plundering Jerusalem.)

3. Skim Nehemiah 4–6. **Compare the tactics used by Sanballat and Tobiah to hinder the construction process with the tactics used by some people today to hinder Christians from doing God's work.** (Sanballat and Tobiah made fun of and mocked the Israelites by insulting their efforts in front of others [4:1-3]. They planned a raid to attack Jerusalem and stop the rebuilding [4:7, 8]. They plotted to harm Nehemiah by requesting to meet with him [6:1, 2]. They made up a phony letter, stating that Nehemiah was plotting to become king of Judah, thus being guilty of treason against the king of Persia [6:6-8]. They hired a false prophet to try to frighten Nehemiah, by saying that men were coming to kill him and that he should go into hiding, thus stopping work on the walls [6:10].)

4. **What can we learn about Nehemiah based on his responses to the various plots and schemes of Sanballat and Tobiah?** (Nehemiah was so focused on the project at hand—the rebuilding of the walls—that he would not allow outside threats—even threats to his life—to interrupt him.)

5. If you had been in Nehemiah's position, how do you think you would have responded to the threats and schemes of Sanballat and Tobiah? Which threat or scheme would have affected you the most? Why?

6. Nehemiah did not halt the construction of the walls when Sanballat and Tobiah were making their threats. So why do you think he stopped construction when the problems among the Israelites became known (5:1-11)? (Perhaps he knew that internal conflict would be much more damaging to the construction process than external conflict.)

7. **Why were the poor Jewish people so upset at their wealthier brothers** (5:1-5)? (This seems to be a case of "the rich getting richer and the poor getting poorer" during a time of crisis. The poor people were paying so much interest on their loans that there seemed to be no way for them to become financially settled again.)

8. **If you were Nehemiah, how would you have handled this internal conflict?** Compare group members' responses with Nehemiah's response in Nehemiah 5:6-13.

9. **Have you ever been in a group or on a team that had to deal with internal conflicts or dissension among the members? If so, what was it like? How did it affect the spirit of the group or team? How was the situation resolved? What were the consequences?**

10. **What can we learn from Nehemiah's leadership example in Nehemiah 5:14–6:14?**

Hand out copies of the reproducible sheet, "Stand Firm," which asks group members to determine how firmly they would stand when faced with opposition in several difficult situations. After a few minutes, ask volunteers to share their responses. Then have group members identify one area in their life in which they're currently facing some opposition. Give them a few minutes to silently take that area to the Lord in prayer, asking Him to help them follow Nehemiah's example in dealing with opposition.

How well do you stand up to opposition? Below are some difficult situations that may test your resolve a little bit. Mark the appropriate box to indicate what you think would be the "strength of your stand" in each situation. Answer honestly—no one else will see your responses if you don't want to share them.

	Call Me Mr./Ms. JELL-O	Wobbling Like a Weeble	Standing, but Swaying	Not Budging an Inch
1. You and some of your fellow youth group members suggest some changes—including singing more contemporary songs and using drama—to "liven up" your church's worship service. A group of older church members get upset at your suggestions and take their complaints to the church board. The board calls a special meeting for you to defend your suggestions.	❏	❏	❏	❏
2. A couple of guys in your English class notice that you carry a Bible with you at school. They start to mock you, calling you "Miss Christian" or "God-boy."	❏	❏	❏	❏
3. You've got a big foreign language exam tomorrow that you're studying for. There's a whole group of kids that you've studied with all year, and you're prepared to cram with them until the library closes. But then one of the kids pulls out a sheet of paper and explains that he found a copy of the test on the teacher's desk and copied the answers while she was out of the room. Everyone starts getting excited about not having to study anymore.	❏	❏	❏	❏
4. The guy/girl that you're really interested in has finally started noticing you. Meaningful glances and shy waves have been passing between the two of you all week. Finally, on Friday afternoon, the two of you decide to go out. You've heard that this person isn't afraid to "circle the bases," but you really wanted to be liked by him/her.	❏	❏	❏	❏
5. After youth group Wednesday night, you and a bunch of your fellow members head for the local pizza joint, where you get into a fairly serious discussion about the youth leader's message. Just then, some of your non-church friends walk in and sit at your table, smelling of smoke and alcohol. They start talking about a new club they found that doesn't check for ID's. They ask you if you want to go with them to the club on Friday night.	❏	❏	❏	❏

A Celebration of Sorts

OVERVIEW

After fifty-two days of construction, the walls of Jerusalem are finally rebuilt. To mark this momentous occasion, the Israelites prepare a celebration to give thanks to God, to repent of their past sins and the past sins of their ancestors, and to plan for the future. The Book of Nehemiah ends with Nehemiah making some final reforms based on the Book of the Law.

OPENING ACT

(Needed: Prizes [optional])

To begin the session, ask several group members to describe the most boring things they've ever had to sit through. Then hand out copies of the reproducible sheet, "Boredom Breakers." Let group members work in pairs or small groups to complete the sheet. After a few minutes, have each pair or small group share its responses. Afterward, ask: **On a scale of one to ten, how boring do you think it would be to stand for five or six hours to listen to someone read a bunch of laws and rules?** Point out that that's exactly what the Israelites did in Nehemiah 8.

DATE I USED THIS SESSION _____ GROUP I USED IT WITH _____

NOTES FOR NEXT TIME _____

_____

_____

1. How long does your average church service last? What's the longest one you've ever sat through? What would you say is the ideal length for a church service? Why?

2. If you were told that you had to sit though a sermon that lasted from daybreak until noon (8:3), how would you respond? Why?

3. Of all of the Israelites' reactions to Ezra's reading of the Book of the Law (8:6-12), which do you find most curious? Why? (The Israelites lifted their hands [8:6], bowed down with their faces on the ground [8:6], wept [8:9], feasted [8:12], sent gifts to the poor [8:12], and celebrated [8:12].)

4. What do you think each of these outward actions demonstrated about what was going on in the people's hearts? (Lifting their hands demonstrated their praise to God. Bowing showed their humility toward God's power. Weeping showed their overwhelming sorrow that their sin had brought such ruin in the first place. Feasting and sending gifts reminded them of how abundantly God had provided for them.)

5. There's an old song that says, "It's my party and I'll cry if I want to." That song certainly could have applied to the Israelites' celebration. Nehemiah and the Levites had to encourage the people to stop weeping and start partying (8:9-11). Why do you think there were such contradictory emotions at this event? (There was sorrow over both the sin that God's Word was pointing out in their lives and for the captivity they had fallen into due to their disobedience. But there was cause to celebrate because God had graciously enabled them to rebuild the walls against all odds and because God was still showing them kindness.)

6. Have you ever been in a situation in which you've had reason to party, but felt like crying instead? If so, what were the circumstances? What happened? Why?

7. How might God's forgiveness, grace, and mercy toward us make us feel both sad and joyful at the same time? How do you think God wants us to respond to His forgiveness, grace, and mercy? Explain.

8. **Why do you think the Israelites were instructed to make booths to live in?** See Leviticus 23:33-44. (It was a remembrance of the living conditions of the Israelites who were delivered from captivity in Egypt.)

9. **If you'd been one of the Israelites, which of the historical events mentioned in the prayer of confession (9:5-37) would have meant most to you? Why?**

10. **Why do you think the Israelites put their "binding agreement" to God in writing?** (Perhaps so that they would have something tangible to refer to later.) **What are some areas of your life in which you might want to establish a binding agreement with God—and perhaps even put it in writing?**

(Needed: Tape, hymnals)

Hand out several pieces of paper and a pencil to each group member. Instruct each person to write down on each sheet one thing that God has done for him or her. See how many sheets your group members can fill. After a few minutes, tape the sheets to the wall like bricks. See how big a "wall" you can create with your group members' sheets. Afterward, give your group members an opportunity to praise God—in a corporate worship setting—for His work in their lives. As a group, sing some hymns that deal with God's forgiveness, grace, and mercy toward us. Among the hymns you might consider using are "Wonderful Grace of Jesus," "Amazing Grace," and "Great Is Thy Faithfulness."

Below are four potentially boring situations. Complete the lists by coming up with some creative and funny suggestions for relieving boredom in each situation.

BOREDOM BREAKERS

TOP FIVE WAYS TO RELIEVE BOREDOM DURING MATH CLASS AT SCHOOL

1. Use your math skills to figure out how many seconds are left in class.

2.

3.

4.

5.

TOP FIVE WAYS TO RELIEVE BOREDOM DURING A DULL SUNDAY SCHOOL LESSON

1. Ask a question from Song of Songs; watch your teacher squirm.

2.

3.

4.

5.

TOP FIVE WAYS TO RELIEVE BOREDOM DURING A LONG CAR TRIP

1. See how many restroom stops you can cause by describing things like a waterfall, a rushing river, a dripping faucet, etc.

2.

3.

4.

5.

TOP FIVE WAYS TO RELIEVE BOREDOM DURING A FAMILY REUNION

1. Stage a contest with another family member to see who can go the longest without being hugged by one of your aunts.

2.

3.

4.

5.

ESTHER 1–4

Queen Search

During a royal celebration, King Xerxes of Persia sends for Queen Vashti to show off her beauty to his guests. When Vashti refuses to come, the king banishes her forever. Thus begins the search for a new queen. After a year-long beauty contest, a Jewish girl named Esther is chosen as queen. However, Esther does not reveal her nationality on the advice of her cousin, Mordecai. Mordecai overhears a plot to assassinate the king and tells Esther about it. Esther, in turn, tells the king, who has the conspirators executed. Haman, the second-in-command behind the king, proposes a law that will result in the execution of all Jewish people. King Xerxes, unaware that Esther is Jewish, passes the law. Mordecai begs Esther to talk to the king on behalf of the Jewish people.

(Needed: Chairs, large bedsheet, prizes)

Stage a beauty contest—featuring kids' toes. Have contestants take off their shoes and socks and stand on chairs behind a large bedsheet. Lift the sheet so that the peoples' toes are the only part of their body that can be seen. Appoint judges to award prizes for categories like hairiest toe, nicest pedicure, longest toe, longest toenail, and so forth. Afterward, point out that the story of Esther involves a beauty contest as well.

DATE I USED THIS SESSION _____ GROUP I USED IT WITH _____

NOTES FOR NEXT TIME _____

_____

_____

1. Have you ever been in a situation in which a lot of people were depending on you? If so, what were the circumstances? How did you feel about the situation? What was the result?

2. Do you think the king's request to Queen Vashti was out of line (1:10, 11)? Why or why not?

3. Why do you think Queen Vashti refused the king's request (1:12)? (Perhaps she didn't enjoy being put on display.) Why do you think the king was so upset when Vashti refused to appear? (Perhaps he felt that he'd been embarrassed in front of his guests.)

4. What do you think of the circumstances surrounding Esther's selection as queen—especially her serving in the king's harem and her reluctance to identify herself as a Jew (2:8-17)? If no one mentions it, point out that part of the mystery of God's sovereignty is that even in imperfect situations, He is at work.

5. Based on the information in Esther 2 and 4, how would you describe Mordecai? Does he remind you of anyone you know today? If so, who? Explain.

6. What character flaws do you see in Haman that might explain why he was so dangerous (Esther 3)? (He was proud, quick-tempered, vengeful, and prone to hold grudges.)

7. Have you ever been involved in or heard of a situation in which someone's "thirst for revenge" got completely out of hand? If so, what were the circumstances? What happened? How did you feel about it? Explain.

8. How do you think Esther felt when she received the message from Mordecai regarding Haman's plans (4:4-17)?

9. In Persian culture, the penalty for appearing before the king without being summoned—and not being received—was death. With this in mind, how do you think Esther first responded when Mordecai asked her to plead her case before the king? What other factors did she have to consider? (The king did not know that she was a Jew.)

10. If you'd been in Esther's position, what would you have done? Why?

11. What's the biggest risk you've ever taken? How did you feel before taking the risk? How did you feel while you were actually taking the risk? How did you feel afterward?

12. Although Esther 1–4 doesn't mention God at all, what are some ways in which God was obviously at work in Esther's life? (First, He gave Esther the beauty that would attract the king [2:7]. He placed Mordecai in a position to uncover the plot to assassinate the king [2:19-23]. Perhaps He prompted Mordecai to counsel Esther to hide the fact that she was Jewish [2:10].)

(Needed: Prizes [optional])

Hand out copies of the reproducible sheet, "Cast of Characters." Give group members a few minutes to record their observations. To motivate kids to write down their observations, you might offer prizes for things like the most unique observation, the weirdest thought, the most observations, the most comical observation, etc. Afterward, have each group member share his or her observations on each character. Then, as a group, try to predict how the story of Esther will turn out, based on group members' observations on each character. Encourage group members to make a special effort to come to your next session to find out "the rest of the story."

Cast of Characters

Below are some of the "featured characters" in the story of Esther. **Jot down as many observations as you can think of regarding each character.** The observations don't necessarily have to be serious or spiritual; they may be as humorous or as off-the-wall as you wish. **Also, if you were a Hollywood casting director working on a movie about Esther, who would you cast in each of the four major roles?**

KING XERXES

HAMAN

MORDECAI

ESTHER

ESTHER 5–10

Oh, What a Tangled Web We Weave . . .

Haman is forced to honor Mordecai, his mortal enemy, for Mordecai's role in saving the king's life five years earlier. As revenge for this humiliation, Haman orders that gallows be built on which to hang Mordecai. Esther invites King Xerxes and Haman to dinner, where she reveals Haman's evil plan to execute all Jewish people. King Xerxes is so outraged that he orders Haman to be hung on the gallows built for Mordecai. Esther and Mordecai then get the king to issue another edict, which, in effect, cancels out Haman's plot to kill the Jews.

(Needed: Several lengths of rope, prizes)

Have kids form teams. Hand each team a length of rope. Give teams one minute to tangle up their rope as much as possible. Then have the teams exchange ropes. Award a prize to the team that untangles its rope first. Hand out copies of the reproducible sheet, "Web of Intrigue." After a few minutes, ask volunteers to share what they came up with—but don't give the correct answers yet. Encourage kids to refer to the sheet periodically as you go through the Bible study.

DATE I USED THIS SESSION _____ GROUP I USED IT WITH _____

NOTES FOR NEXT TIME _____

_____

_____

1. Have you ever allowed other people to think that you're someone that you're really not? We're not just talking about identities here. Have you ever allowed someone to believe that you had a different personality, background, or interests than you really did? If so, why did you do it?

2. Read Esther 5:1-6. **Put yourself in Esther's shoes. You have a secret identity as a Jew that your husband, the king, knows nothing about. You have an enemy, Haman, who has plotted to kill all of your people, but does not realize that you are one of them. You invite both of them to a meal. What are you thinking and feeling while you prepare the food? Explain.**

3. **Why do you think Esther avoided answering the king's question during the first banquet and waited until the second banquet to tell him what she wanted** (5:1-8)? (Perhaps she couldn't work up the courage. Perhaps she wanted to build the king's suspense and eagerness.)

4. **Based on Esther 5:9-14, how would you describe Haman?** (Arrogant, proud, easily offended, boastful, insensitive, wealthy, petty, and vengeful.) **What do you suppose King Xerxes saw in Haman to give him such an exalted position?**

5. **Using facial expressions and body language only, how do you think Haman reacted when he thought the king wanted to honor him** (6:6)? **How do you think Haman reacted when he found out that it was Mordecai, Haman's arch enemy, that the king wanted to honor** (6:10)?

6. **How do you think King Xerxes responded when he discovered that Esther was Jewish** (7:4)? **How do you think Haman responded when he discovered the same thing?**

7. **What lessons can we learn from Haman's life and death? Explain.**

8. If King Xerxes had given you the authority to make any decree you wish, what would you have done? Compare group members' responses with the decree Mordecai came up with in Esther 8:10-13.

9. At the end of the Book of Esther, the Israelites are at peace, having conquered their enemies; Mordecai, a godly leader, is second in command to King Xerxes. How long do you think it will be before the Isralites mess up their situation again by disobeying God again? Explain.

10. God is never mentioned in the Book of Esther. Do you see anything in the book to indicate that God was working in the lives of Esther and Mordecai? If so, what? And if so, why do you think the book neglects to mention God?

11. What can we learn from the story of Esther regarding situations that seem to be hopeless?

(Needed: Guest speaker)

Follow up the last question by having group members pair up—preferably with a friend or someone they know relatively well. Ask each person to share with his or her partner a situation that he or she is facing that seems to be hopeless. Then have the partners offer each other encouragement. Close the session in prayer, asking God to demonstrate His power in the lives of your group members facing "hopeless" situations. (If possible, you might also want to bring in an expert on Judaism to explain the significance of the Purim celebration to Jewish people today.)

Web of INTRIGUE

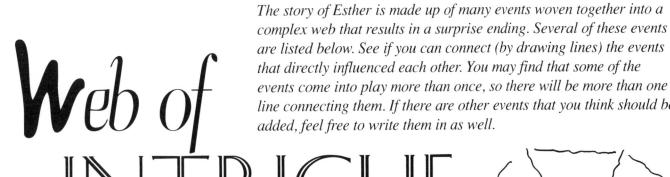

The story of Esther is made up of many events woven together into a complex web that results in a surprise ending. Several of these events are listed below. See if you can connect (by drawing lines) the events that directly influenced each other. You may find that some of the events come into play more than once, so there will be more than one line connecting them. If there are other events that you think should be added, feel free to write them in as well.

Mordecai foils an assassination plot.

Haman plots revenge.

Haman is hanged.

Esther hides her nationality.

Mordecai is honored.

Esther hosts a small dinner party.

Haman develops a hatred for Mordecai and all other Jewish people.

The Jewish people are saved.

Haman desires honor and power.

Esther becomes queen.

Esther reveals her identity and Haman's scheme.

The king has trouble sleeping.